The Nature
of Nurture

biology, environment and the drug-exposed child

———— ꙮ ꙮ ————

The Nature of Nurture:
Biology, Environment and the Drug-Exposed Child

Ira J. Chasnoff, M.D.

NTI Publishing

Chicago

The Nature of Nurture: Biology, Environment and the Drug-Exposed Child

Published by NTI Publishing

http://www.cr-triangle.org/nti

Edited by Arthur Wildbrew

Instructional Design and illustrations by Wei C. Hung, Ph.D.

Cover Design by Wei C. Hung, Ph.D.

Print & Binding by Exponent Publishers, Inc.

This book is printed on acid-free paper.

Library of Congress Catalog Card Number: 2001086001

ISBN 0-9707762-0-9

To Naomi and Rudy...

*who proved that love and commitment
can make all the difference.*

Contents

contents, *cont.*

contents, *cont.*

contents, *cont.*

Foreword

As addiction continues to tear families apart, growing numbers of children are being left to fight for survival in an already overcrowded foster care system. Now, 80% of children reported to child protection services across the nation have been removed from their homes because of drug and alcohol problems in the family. At the same time, more than half of the mothers placing their babies for adoption through private adoption agencies have used alcohol or illegal drugs during the pregnancy. So in both the public and private sectors, foster and adoptive parents are left to pick up the pieces and to restore sanity and calm to the children's lives.

Unfortunately, foster and adoptive parents are receiving inadequate and often confusing information about the children they bring into their homes. We all recognize that children who have been prenatally exposed to drugs or alcohol can suffer a wide range of physical and behavioral problems. But, on the other hand, data coming out of research and clinical programs consistently show that, with intervention, drug- and alcohol-exposed children can succeed in school and in long-term development. Recent interviews with twenty foster and adoptive families regarding their experience in obtaining information about drug-exposed children revealed the depth of confusion that exists:

- Six of the twenty families had been told by a physician not to have the child immunized because of neurological risk from the effects of prenatal exposure to cocaine.

- Four physicians, despite having no information on the drug-using birth mother's HIV status, stated that HIV testing need not be considered because the child was not at risk of exposure prenatally.

- Sixteen of the families had been warned by a physician not to bring a prenatally exposed child into their home because of the severe damage, especially to cognitive and behavioral functioning, done by prenatal alcohol and drug exposure.

Such misinformation provided to parents on the one hand discourages foster care and adoption of children labeled as drug-exposed and on the other hand impedes the delivery of appropriate interventions to this special population of children. School systems take unnecessary steps to identify drug-exposed children without looking beyond the child's label to guide the development of programs and learning strategies that can best address the needs of the child. In spite of these difficulties, families continue to adopt and care for drug- and alcohol-exposed children, convinced that with enough love, they can overcome any obstacles. But it takes more than love. It takes knowledge, skills, and persistence.

The purpose of this book is to provide foster and adoptive parents, teachers, and health care and social service professionals with the information they need to help children achieve the behavior and developmental skills necessary for success in school and beyond. The case studies that are used throughout the book to illustrate important points are based on actual children and families who have been seen at the Child Study Center, our clinical center for the evaluation and treatment of high-risk children and their families. Children do not come with a map. And we cannot give you a recipe for growth or a series of "tips" that will help you control your child. But we can provide you with a practical approach to *managing* your child's behavior that is based in theory, proven through research, and grounded in experience.

The journey to parenthood is a difficult one, but one gladly undertaken every day by foster and adoptive parents. This book is dedicated to those parents, the first teachers and strongest advocates for children who too many times have been left behind in a rush to judgment.

Ira J. Chasnoff, M.D.
January 1, 2001

Tears ran down his cheeks, falling on the math paper like tiny glimmering raindrops. I looked sidewise at him. He held his body rigid as he fought to keep control. "What's the matter Mike?" I asked. His kept his head low, ashamed for me to see him cry, and in a voice I could hardly hear, "I can't do this." "Yes, you can!" I said, "You can do it, I know you can. We just have to keep on." He did a few more problems, guessing wildly. I kept my voice low and calm, "Put the number here. Multiply, subtract, bring down the next number...yes that's it. You can do it." A few more problems. I kept talking, "Multiply, subtract, bring down the next number, what is the remainder.... You can do it, keep trying. " Five or six more problems repeating steadily and quietly, "You can do it." He was starting to relax, and his answers were making more sense. He lifted his face. "I get it, Susan," he cried. "I get it! I can do the rest on my own."

Mike is my brother. He came to us when he was only a few weeks old, and now he is twelve. This is just another day in his life. Tests show that he is as smart as other kids, but he takes a little longer to learn and he needs more time to finish his work. He has been affected by a few thoughtless acts that took place before he was even born. His mom used cocaine when she was pregnant. She really didn't mean any harm; she was just partying and having fun. The drugs crossed the placenta when the brain was being formed and affected the neurotransmitters. Mom got over it. The baby did not.

Every day I watch my brother struggle to function in a predictable organized way. He has difficulty controlling his behavior, becomes over stimulated easily and loses control. As a baby, we would wrap him tightly in a blanket and rock him to soothe him. At four Mike was playing with friends when I heard someone scream, "Mike bit me." I started to put him in time out, but the look of horror and confusion on his face stopped me. I realized how frightened he was by his own behavior and how powerless he felt to stop it.

Mike lives with the effects of drug exposure on a daily basis. No amount of rehabilitation will make it go completely away. When I take him to school, I see his body stiffen as he goes to face the tests that he will not be able to finish and the problems he will struggle to understand. And when I see the tears falling down his cheeks, I fight to hold back my rage at all those who choose that moment of pleasure over the welfare of their unborn children. I keep my voice steady, "You can do it, you can do it, yes you can."

Susan, age 17

CHAPTER 1

Risk and Protective Factors in the Life of a Child

A child's development is a dynamic process, involving both social and biological factors that contribute to success or failure. From day one, the child interacts with the environment around him and seeks the nurturing support that will help him achieve his full potential. We know, of course, that genetic patterns have a strong impact on intellectual development, behavior, mental health, and educational achievement, but the environment in which the child is being raised shapes ultimate outcome.

The majority of children in the child welfare system are there because of drug or alcohol problems in the family. As they come to their foster and adoptive homes, they present with two immediate risk factors: early separation from their family and exposure to drugs and alcohol during pregnancy. Multiple additional risk factors - a home in which substance abuse and mental health disorders interfered with the way the family functioned, lack of adequate health care, poor access to developmental services, unsafe environments, prolonged placement in the foster care system - compound the tragedy. During the critical early years of life these high-risk and vulnerable children often were not provided with the support and positive opportunities they needed to develop the knowledge, skills, and behaviors essential for their long-term development and achievement.

Mental health and social issues in the birth family

The drug-exposed child most often comes from a neglectful family lifestyle filled with factors that interfere with the biological parents' attempts at effective child rearing and participation in the growth and development of their children. These factors are present to some extent in all women who abuse drugs at a high level, regardless of economic status. Further, the social environment of many addicted women is one of chaos and instability, which has an even greater negative impact on children.

Addicted women frequently have poor family and social support networks, have few positive relationships with other women, and often are dependent on an unreliable, abusive male, thereby increasing their vulnerability to physical and sexual abuse. In turn, children of substance-abusing women are at greater risk for neglect and sexual, physical, and psychological harm. These difficulties are magnified in children living in poverty, because their mothers frequently lack the social and economic supports that could help alleviate some of the social isolation as well as the biological impact of prenatal drug exposure.

Significant psychiatric problems such as a personality disorder or depression, are not uncommon in women who use drugs or abuse alcohol. These factors almost invariably hinder parenting capabilities further and lessen the chance for a normal developmental course for the child. Even in depressed women who do not use drugs or alcohol, there is less involvement with their children, poor communication among family members, increased friction, lack of affection, and an increase in guilt and resentment toward the child. To further complicate the picture, children of depressed mothers are much more likely to be depressed themselves, and the cycle of depression and drug use continues across the generations.

Foster care and adoption

Although the child welfare system has usually been the refuge for endangered children, in the past ten years the system has become overwhelmed. Drug and alcohol abuse is among the most commonly named factors cited as contributing to the increase in child maltreatment, and almost all States report that substance abuse is the dominant characteristic in child protective service caseloads. By 1990, the influx of drug-exposed infants into a system that already had a short supply of foster homes had stretched the substitute care system to its breaking point. Families that seek adoption through private agencies cannot avoid these problems. It is estimated that among babies available for private adoption domestically, slightly over half their mothers used alcohol or illegal drugs during pregnancy.

Children in the foster care system have a wide variety of health problems that can have an impact on their long-term outcome. In addition to their prenatal drug or alcohol exposure, their poor health is a reflection of poverty, family and neighborhood violence, and multiple placements in a variety of foster families. As a result, foster children frequently have not received their immunizations nor had the routine health care required for ultimate growth. Anemia, Sickle Cell Disease, growth delays, lead poisoning, repeated ear infections, sexually transmitted diseases, asthma and chronic diarrhea often complicate the picture and have gone undetected or unattended.

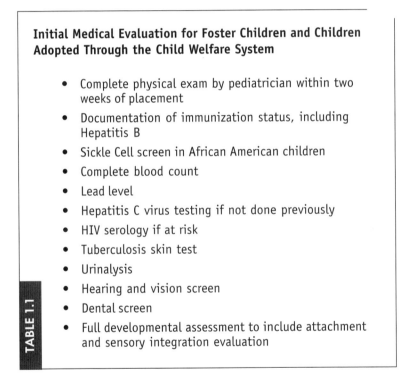

Initial Medical Evaluation for Foster Children and Children Adopted Through the Child Welfare System

- Complete physical exam by pediatrician within two weeks of placement
- Documentation of immunization status, including Hepatitis B
- Sickle Cell screen in African American children
- Complete blood count
- Lead level
- Hepatitis C virus testing if not done previously
- HIV serology if at risk
- Tuberculosis skin test
- Urinalysis
- Hearing and vision screen
- Dental screen
- Full developmental assessment to include attachment and sensory integration evaluation

TABLE 1.1

Attachment

Human attachment and care giving are as essential to our species' continued existence as nourishment and reproduction. At the core of human survival is the protection of the younger, smaller and weaker members of the species by those older and stronger. It is through this essential relationship that a child's expectations for relationships with others are developed and trust evolves. Unfortunately, national studies reveal that children placed in foster care due to parental substance abuse, as compared to children placed for other reasons, are separated from their mothers earlier, stay in out-of-home placements longer, experience more changes in placement, are less likely to return home, and have lower rates of adoption. This is particularly true for children of color. Children living in institutions suffer this same pattern of displacement and loss.

Early separation from an infant's mother or the absence of a consistent, loving caregiver are among the most profoundly damaging blows an infant's psyche can experience. It is through this essential first relationship that the infant's positive development begins. Infants develop their sense of trust in the first years of life. This sense of trust is developed through loving and reciprocal interactions with a consistent caregiver. Ultimately, all young children require an essential reciprocal relationship with at least one adult who is fully committed to the child. Without this relationship, the child's capacity for positive self-esteem and love for others can never develop.

Infants who do not receive a reciprocal smile or acceptance from parents will internalize this rejection as shame, often manifest through depression and attachment problems. However, children who are securely attached to their caregiver feel safe and secure, emotionally stable and "inoculated" from further difficulties during the course of their development.

Children in foster care often do not have the opportunity to develop the kind of attachments they need to thrive. Early placement in the child welfare system, multiple placements, and prolonged wandering from one family to the next results in the child not knowing his place in life and having no one upon whom he can rely. In a study of 64 foster children in Chicago, it was found that developmental scores for most of the children fell in the mildly delayed range. Evaluation of behavior of the children revealed a significant number of behavioral problems, including distractibility, short attention span, impulsive behavior, anxiety and depression, and difficulty staying on track. Clinical assessment of the children revealed that the 24 children age three months to three years had a problem controlling their behavior. In addition, three of the children had a reactive attachment disorder, and two of the children exhibited signs of traumatic stress disorder. Among the 40 children ages four to five years, four met criteria for Attention Deficit Hyperactivity Disorder, and another four had a reactive attachment disorder. Three additional children met criteria for an adjustment disorder, and another two children had a diagnosis of post- traumatic stress disorder. Thus it can be seen that these foster children were bringing significant behavioral and mental health problems with them as they entered foster care.

Overseas adoption

Attachment issues are of special concern when families adopt from overseas, a practice that has become much more common over the past ten years. In 1998 alone, U.S. citizens adopted a total of almost 16,000 children from foreign countries. The number of children adopted from Russia especially has grown, nearly doubling since 1986. In the past two years, Americans have adopted more children from Russia than any other country.

Political unrest and a failing economy have led many Russian families into poverty. These families frequently are unable to care for their children and place them in institutions to relieve themselves of the financial demands of having a young child. Placement into an orphanage also is a common practice when the State rescinds parental rights due to alcohol or drug addiction, criminal behavior, or unusual religious practices.

The living conditions for the children in orphanages around the world are subsistent at best, compounding the significant neglect, abuse, and malnutrition they usually suffered prior to their placement. The children receive substandard medical attention delivered by untrained staff, if they receive any sort of care at all. Medical records are incomplete, difficult to translate and subject to variance based on the cultural bias of the country of origin. It is customary in countries from the former Soviet Union to subscribe to a system with a foundation laid in pathology, and during their first few years of life children are considered "neurologically immature."

Rickets and anemia are extremely common among children adopted from orphanages overseas. These illnesses can cause growth delays, developmental delays, kidney dysfunction, and learning problems. Due to the lack of medical care and the neglect suffered in the orphanages, many of the children throw themselves into a mode of survival that inhibits their ability to grow, causing failure to thrive, poor brain growth, and developmental delays. However, growth can "catch up" over time, given the right conditions, and, while initial growth parameters of the children are below normal when they arrive in the United States, significant improvements are noted once the children are placed in a nurturing environment.

Diagnoses of Fetal Alcohol Syndrome (FAS) and Fetal Alcohol Effect (FAE) are increasingly common among Russian orphans. In 1980, the Academy of Sciences reported that there were 40 million registered alcoholics in a Russian population of 260 million. Based on a review of pre-adoptive evaluations conducted between 1994 and 1997, some researchers have estimated that 15 of every 1,000 babies born in Russia receive a diagnosis of FAS. It is probable that these figures have continued to increase over the past three years.

The lack of interaction and stimulation that the institutionalized infants endure and the restricted movement that results from the customary swaddling of babies produce infants with significant developmental delays and severe abnormalities of muscle tone. As infants, it is not uncommon to find that motor development and speech and language development have not moved beyond the three month developmental level, even in children as old as 18 months.

In addition, Russian orphans often are subjected to aversive conditions during their institutionalization. These conditions further exacerbate delays in development and restrict opportunities for a normal life. In the orphanages, the children frequently receive a diagnosis of "oligophrenia." This diagnosis is assigned to children with emotional and behavioral difficulties or "mental handicaps." Children diagnosed as oligophrenic cannot attend mainstream classes, are deprived of basic civil rights, may not pursue employment of their choice, and have little chance of altering their diagnosis. They are separated from society at large in their residency and employment.

Families who adopt from overseas face many challenges, but these challenges are similar in many ways to those associated with domestic adoption. Although only early research information is now available, it does appear that children adopted from overseas can thrive and succeed with the right interventions and support in their early years as they transition to life in a nurturing and supportive home.

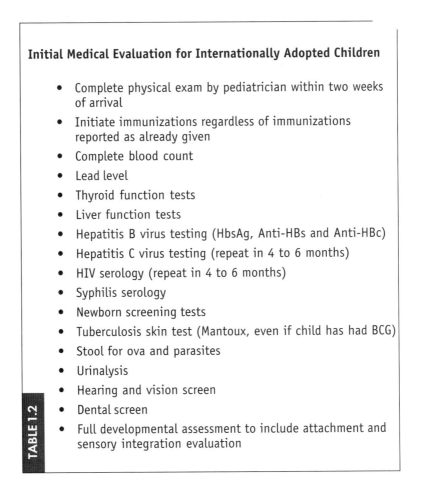

Initial Medical Evaluation for Internationally Adopted Children

- Complete physical exam by pediatrician within two weeks of arrival
- Initiate immunizations regardless of immunizations reported as already given
- Complete blood count
- Lead level
- Thyroid function tests
- Liver function tests
- Hepatitis B virus testing (HbsAg, Anti-HBs and Anti-HBc)
- Hepatitis C virus testing (repeat in 4 to 6 months)
- HIV serology (repeat in 4 to 6 months)
- Syphilis serology
- Newborn screening tests
- Tuberculosis skin test (Mantoux, even if child has had BCG)
- Stool for ova and parasites
- Urinalysis
- Hearing and vision screen
- Dental screen
- Full developmental assessment to include attachment and sensory integration evaluation

TABLE 1.2

Stress in adoptive parents

The path to adoption often is strewn with disappointments, uncertain timetables, unremitting stress, and unfulfilled expectations. Many adoptive couples choose the path of adoption primarily due to infertility. This in itself can create problems, including depression, reduced self-esteem, anxiety, and a breakdown in communication and sexual activity. If left unresolved, these difficulties can undermine family relations. The excitement of finally creating a family can create high expectations in adoptive parents for both the child and the parent-child relationship, even when the parents have knowledge of their adoptive child's poor state of health. Deflated expectations can then produce a stress on the family system and inhibit the growth and development, particularly healthy attachment relationships, of children even though they have been placed in a more stable environment. Parents who enter adoption understanding and acknowledging the difficulties they may face will enhance their child's ultimate emotional and physical health.

Risk and resiliency

The healthy infant is born with sound developmental capabilities that are augmented by life circumstances. However, as the child grows and develops, she is vulnerable to a variety of *risk factors* that can negatively affect long-term outcome. As the number of risk factors builds, risk for the child's ultimate outcome increases significantly. *Protective factors* modify the child's response to environmental hazards, and *resiliency* is the capacity to adapt after being exposed to stressful events. The child's inborn biological resilience or resilience developed through emotional and developmental support in the home allow the infant to meet challenges and overcome adversity.

This concept of the balance of risk and resiliency can guide our understanding of the biological and environmental factors that affect the foster or adopted child's development. However, it cannot predict ultimate outcome of the child, since the child's development is an ongoing process shaped by multiple factors, many of which interact and influence one another in ways we cannot mea- sure. On the other hand, we do know that intervention strategies that

- address multiple risk factors rather than focusing on only one factor;
- provide the child and family support in a variety of settings;
- work with the family and child for two to five years; and
- are initiated as early as possible in the infant's life

have the greatest potential for positively affecting the outcome of the child. These tenets are the foundation upon which we have built our approach to working with high risk children.

The role of the family

Most current information emerging about the effects of prenatal drug exposure on infants and children raises a critical issue: the role of the family environment in improving the biologically deter-mined effects of prenatal substance exposure. Longitudinal research has shown that the way in which a family functions is an extremely important factor in predicting how children behave. However, dis-tortion in the media of long-term outcomes for prenatally exposed children and misinformation in the medical setting has painted a bleak picture that has frightened foster families and caused poten-tial adoptive families to back away from accepting the children into their home.

To complicate matters even more, parents who bring foster or adoptive children into their homes frequently confront health and child mental health systems that are not prepared to provide the intensive, comprehensive services that many of the children need. Further, in most States in this country, infants without documented developmental delays are not, for the most part, eligible for early intervention programs. Since substance-exposed infants often do not demonstrate such delays, early intervention programs will not serve them. Thus, the infants from an early age face numerous risks for mental health problems that escalate over time, but they have access to few services to address these risks. In stark contrast, there is clear evidence that early intervention significantly improves the outcome of the child prenatally exposed to drugs or alcohol. This is the dilemma foster and adoptive parents face as they seek services for their children.

The role of the foster or adoptive family thus boils down to a complex mix of advocacy, consistency, and support for the child and her needs. Whether it is in the context of obtaining adequate health care, developmental interventions, or educational services, the parents often find themselves educating the professionals who should be serving their child. In these situations, information is the parents' strongest weapon. The following chapters will first explore the impact prenatal exposure to alcohol and illegal drugs has on the child's long-term health, development, behavior, and school achievement. We then will turn our attention to a theoretical and practical approach to behavioral interventions that can promote the child's ultimate success in all aspects of her life.

■   ■   ■

Fetal Alcohol Syndrome

There is a biblical warning against the use of alcohol during pregnancy, and among the ancient Greeks and Romans, alcohol was recognized as a cause of damage to the unborn child. However, despite this early recognition of the problems alcohol consumption can cause, little progress has been made in reducing the rate of alcohol use by pregnant women. In fact, physicians rarely ask a pregnant woman about her alcohol use, and Fetal Alcohol Syndrome remains the most common cause of diagnosable mental retardation in the United States.

Although illegal drug use has garnered most of the media attention in the past few decades, alcohol is a common denominator when evaluating the child who has been exposed to any number of drugs. For this reason, we will separately address the consumption of alcohol during pregnancy and its impact on the developing fetus and child.

Criteria for diagnosis

Fetal Alcohol Syndrome (FAS) is the name given to a cluster of physical and mental defects present from birth that is the direct result of a woman drinking alcoholic beverages while she is pregnant. Infants with Fetal Alcohol Syndrome have signs in three categories:

1. Poor growth

In the United States, the average birth weight of babies born at full term (38 to 42 weeks gestation) is 7 pounds 8 ounces, with a normal range down to 5 pounds 8 ounces. Babies born to mothers who use alcohol have an average birth weight of around 6 pounds and are more likely to weigh less than 5 pounds 8 ounces. In addition, head size of babies with Fetal Alcohol Syndrome is reduced. The average head size of full term infants is 35 cm, while head size of a baby with FAS is less than about 33 cm. As children with FAS grow older, they tend to continue to be small for age, and head size continues to be small.

2. Central nervous system involvement

FAS is the most common cause of diagnosable mental retardation and the only preventable cause. In addition to low I.Q., children with FAS may have learning problems associated with the inability to understand cause and effect relationships and long term consequences. Many of the children have a short attention span, are poorly coordinated, and are hyperactive. They also may have delays in their ability to use language appropriately for their age.

The Newborn Infant: What's Normal?

	Normal	Normal range
Gestation (length of pregnancy)	40 weeks	38-42 weeks
Birth weight at term	7 lb. 8 oz	5 lb. 8 oz – 9 lb. 8 oz.
Birth length at term	20 inches	19" – 22"
Birth head circumference	35 cm	33 cm – 38.5 cm
APGAR scores	7 or above	7 – 10
Daily formula	17 oz.	15 – 20 oz.
Total daily sleep time	16 hours	14 – 18 hours
Longest sleep period	3 – 4 hours	
Longest awake period	2.5 hours	
Time spent crying in a day	2 hours	up to about 3 hours

TABLE 2.1 This chart is provided as a general reference for "what's normal." However, even these figures will vary for the individual child.

3. Typical facial characteristics

Facial features are consistent with overall mid-face hypoplasia; i.e., undergrowth and flattening of the middle portion of the face. As a result, the infants exhibit:

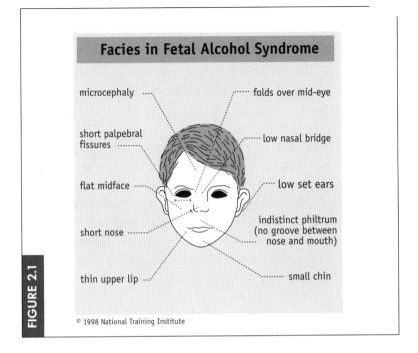

Facies in Fetal Alcohol Syndrome

microcephaly ······

short palpebral fissures ·········

flat midface ········

short nose ········

thin upper lip ···

folds over mid-eye

low nasal bridge

low set ears

indistinct philtrum (no groove between nose and mouth)

small chin

© 1998 National Training Institute

FIGURE 2.1

- microcephaly (small head)
- epicanthal folds (extra skin folds coming down around the inner angle of the eye)
- short palpebral fissures (small eye openings)
- a flattened elongated philtrum (no groove or crease running from the bottom of the nose to the top of the lip),
- thin upper lip
- small mouth with high arched palate (roof of the mouth)
- small teeth with poor enamel coating
- low set ears.

These changes can vary in severity, but usually persist over the life of the child. Most people will not recognize any differences when they see the child, but someone with experience in working with children prenatally exposed to alcohol will be able to detect the changes.

Children with Fetal Alcohol Syndrome also may have a variety of malformations of major organs, especially the heart, kidneys, eyes, and ears. Although not all children with FAS should have a consultation with a heart specialist, the primary care physician should evaluate the heart carefully. Almost all children with FAS have vision problems, with a good number of them having an eye that turns in or a lazy eye. The pediatrician often can easily diagnose this and treat the child initially by patching the eye. However, surgery is sometimes required.

There is an increased rate of kidney malformations such as hydronephrosis (swelling of the kidneys due to obstructed urine flow), horseshoe kidneys and other rotational abnormalities in children with FAS. In addition, children with FAS have a predisposition to ear infections and a high rate of hearing loss (eighth nerve deafness), so a thorough hearing exam is usually beneficial. Because the ears and kidneys form at the same time in the womb, if the child has any abnormalities of the ears or hearing, he should have an ultrasound of the kidneys immediately.

Fetal Alcohol Effects

A child whose mother drank alcohol during pregnancy but who has only partial or no overt expression of physical features of alcohol exposure is said to have Fetal Alcohol Effects (FAE). These children may have minimal to moderate facial changes, or no changes at all, but usually have some problems in mental development. Most importantly, they frequently exhibit behavioral difficulties that have a significant impact on learning and long-term development. FAE usually is not apparent until the child is in a social setting, such as school, and the learning difficulties may not emerge until second or third grade.

Over the past few years, there has been a move to replace the term *Fetal Alcohol Effects* with the more precise phrases, *Alcohol-Related Neurodevelopmental Disorder* (ARND) and *Alcohol-Related Birth Defects* (ARBD)(Table 2.2). ARND is diagnosed when a child has a confirmed or reported exposure to alcohol, demonstrates central nervous system abnormalities, including small head size, and has evidence of a complex pattern of behavior or cognitive abnormalities. ARBD occurs when there is a confirmed history of exposure to alcohol during pregnancy and the child has birth defects associated with alcohol exposure, including defects of the face, heart, bones, kidneys, eyes, or ears. In this context, children exposed prenatally to illicit drugs, such as cocaine or heroin, and who have behavioral or developmental problems, are classified as having a *Drug-Related Neurodevelopmental Disorder* (DRND).

FAS: Fetal Alcohol Syndrome

ARND: Alcohol-Related Neurodevelopmental Disorder

ARBD: Alcohol-Related Birth Defects

DRND: Drug-Related Neurodevelopmental Disorder

● Must be present
● May be present

	FAS	ARND	ARBD	DRND
Documented maternal alcohol use during pregnancy	●	●	●	
Documented maternal illicit drug use during pregnancy				●
Growth patterns Weight _____ lb. _____ oz. ☐ <10% Length _____ inches ☐ <10%	●			●
Facial malformation Epicanthal folds Thin upper lip Flat philtrum Flat mid-face	●	●		
Abnormal neurodevelopment Head circumference _____ cm ☐ <10% Short attention span Increased activity Impulsive behavior Distractibility Easily over-stimulated Difficulty with self-soothing Delayed motor, language, or cognitive development	●	●		●
Malformations Facial Heart Kidneys Ears Limb	●		●	

TABLE 2.2

	Lower Normal Limits (10%)									
	birth		3ms.		6ms.		1 yr.		2 yrs.	
	boys	girls	boys	girls	boys	girls	boys	girls	boys	girls
Wt.	6#	6#	11#	10#	14# 8	13# 8	19# 8	18#	24#	22# 8
Lt.	19"	18.25"	23"	22"	25.5"	24.5"	29"	28"	33"	32.5"
HC.	33cm	33cm	39cm	38cm	42cm	41cm	45cm	44cm	48cm	46.5cm

Information processing in children with FAS or ARND

The behavioral difficulties of children with FAS and ARND can best be understood as a deficit in processing information: recording information, interpreting the information, storing the information for later use, and utilizing the information through appropriate language and motor skills. The drawing of the brain in Figure 2.2 shows the major structures of the brain as well as the sections of the brain primarily responsible for sensation and movement. The surface of the brain, the *cerebral cortex*, is divided into two halves, the right and left hemispheres. Each of the hemispheres is divided into four lobes. The *frontal lobe* on each side of the brain is responsible for the planning, execution and control of movements. The *primary motor cortex* contains nerves that participate in the control of movement. The back lobes of the brain (the *parietal, temporal* and *occipital lobes*) are specialized for perception. The *primary somatosensory cortex* receives information about the body senses: touch, pressure, temperature, and pain. The *primary visual cortex* at the back of the occipital lobes receives visual information, and the *primary auditory cortex* that lies in the temporal lobes receives auditory information.

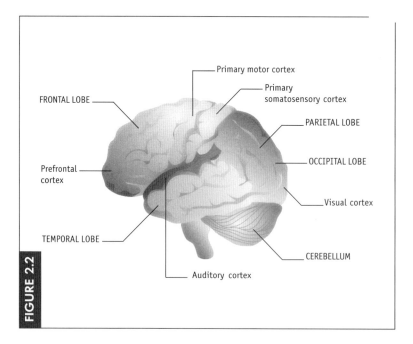

FIGURE 2.2

The rest of the cortex is referred to as *association cortex*, the parts of the brain that link information (Figure 2.3).

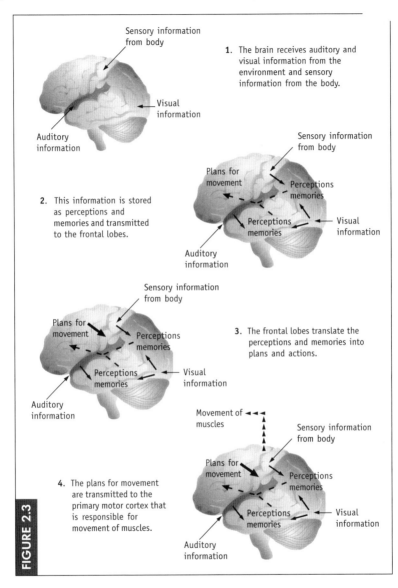

FIGURE 2.3

Sensory information from body

1. The brain receives auditory and visual information from the environment and sensory information from the body.

Visual information

Auditory information

Sensory information from body

Plans for movement

Perceptions memories

2. This information is stored as perceptions and memories and transmitted to the frontal lobes.

Perceptions memories

Visual information

Auditory information

Sensory information from body

Plans for movement

Perceptions memories

3. The frontal lobes translate the perceptions and memories into plans and actions.

Perceptions memories

Visual information

Auditory information

Movement of muscles

Sensory information from body

Plans for movement

Perceptions memories

4. The plans for movement are transmitted to the primary motor cortex that is responsible for movement of muscles.

Perceptions memories

Visual information

Auditory information

For example, the association cortex in the frontal lobes (the *prefrontal cortex*) is involved in the planning of movements and controls the activity of nerves in the primary motor cortex, which in turn controls actual muscle movement. Alcohol-exposed children with damage to the prefrontal cortex have difficulty regulating their behaviors and exhibit poor planning and forethought. They appear to be impulsive, inattentive, and out of control. The primary visual cortex and the primary auditory cortex send information to each respective association cortex to link movement with the senses. If children sustain damage to the visual association cortex, they will not become blind; however, they may be unable to recognize objects by sight, although they can often recognize them if they feel them with their hands. If alcohol damages the somatosensory cortex, the child will have difficulty perceiving the shapes of objects that he can touch but not see. He may be unable to name parts of his body, or he may have trouble drawing maps or following them.

Research has revealed that children who have been exposed to alcohol during pregnancy frequently have changes in the inner layer, or substructure, of the brain (Figure 2.4). This is the area that is responsible for linking and processing information. The *basal ganglia* are undergrown in children who were exposed to alcohol prenatally. The basal ganglia receive input from the cortex to help regulate motor behavior. The functional impact of the basal ganglia's being reduced in volume is still being studied in alcohol-exposed children.

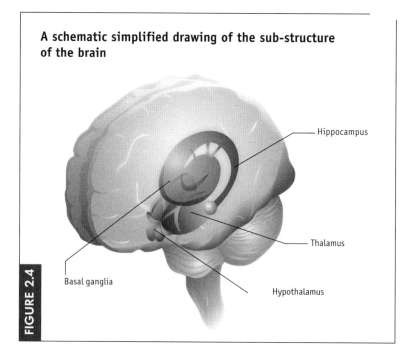

A schematic simplified drawing of the sub-structure of the brain

Hippocampus

Thalamus

Basal ganglia

Hypothalamus

FIGURE 2.4

The *hippocampus* receives information from all regions of the sensory parts of the brain and from the motor cortex of the frontal lobes. Damage to the hippocampus from alcohol exposure may cause learning and memory problems. For example, asking a child to turn on the dishwasher often will result in her going to the kitchen, but she cannot remember what to do when she gets there. Other alcohol-induced structural changes in the brain can occur in the *corpus callosum*, the section of the brain that permits the two major halves of the brain, the *cerebral hemispheres*, to share information. If this communication is interrupted, as it is in alcohol-exposed children, then some types of information may never reach consciousness. For example, a child can recite the rules for good behavior in the school lunchroom, but then cannot understand or follow them. Finally, the *thalamus* receives neural input from all over the body and sends it to the *cerebral cortex*, the area of the brain responsible for cognition and learning. The thalamus helps organize behavior related to survival – fighting, feeding, fleeing. This is why children with FAS or ARND often get a look of panic in their eyes when faced with a sudden change or threat or overloaded with information. Parents describe the children as "not there."

It therefore can be seen that the behaviors demonstrated by children with FAS or ARND are a result of physiologic damage, not willful misconduct. When a child knows all his spelling words one day, and cannot spell a single word the next day, he often is accused of having "selective memory." Instead, the child is having difficulty recording information and storing it for later use. This child will need special, often multi-sensory, cues to be able to remember the spelling words. The child who runs out into the street is not being disobedient. She simply has not made the connection between the words, "Do not run out into the street," and the literal motor action. Thus, she will need clear structure ("This is the boundary of our yard.") to ensure her safety.

These are the issues that have the greatest long-term impact on the children. For the most part, follow up studies of children with FAS have shown that the children have done very poorly. They did not attain independent lives and had severe and complex secondary disabilities. However, these outcomes pertain mainly to children who continued to live in an environment in which alcohol was abused and who often had very little, if any, early intervention services. Children who are adopted into new families, whether foster or adoptive, may have a better outlook than children who stay with their biological parents.

Drugs, Pregnancy and the Growing Child

I met Freddie in 1986. He was sitting on his mother's lap, a robust, full-cheeked six-month-old with the brownest, most knowing eyes I had ever seen in an infant. "There's something wrong." Ruth's voice was strong, her gaze direct.

"Wrong?" I repeated. "He looks fine to me."

"That's what all the other doctors say, but I know different."

There was no denying Ruth, so I listened to her story. Freddie had been born to a mother who showed up one day in the hospital, delivered, and left, never to be seen again. Ruth took Freddie into her home at three days, and he had been living with her since. Experience with her own children and grandchildren had told Ruth right away that something was not right. Freddie was irritable and at times inconsolable. He pulled away from her when she tried to hold him close, and the more she tried the worse he got. There were two episodes when he seemed to "go blank," turning from her and staring at the opposite wall. His feeding was erratic, and although he eventually took in adequate amounts of formula, it took hours to feed him. It seemed that one feeding would run right into the next.

Ruth took Freddie to a series of doctors, but the advice was always the same. "You're too old to be taking care of a new baby. Go home and call DCFS to come get him." Whether out of pity or pure stubbornness, Ruth ignored them all. She heard about our center from another foster mother, wheedled an immediate appointment, and appeared early one morning armed and ready for anyone who tried to turn her away.

During the examination, Freddie lay quietly, giving way to tremors and irritability when I disturbed him. His behavior would escalate rapidly, reaching a peak of crying and shaking, then suddenly quiet into a deep, impenetrable sleep. Ruth's eyes met mine, and I continued my exam.

Freddie's face appeared flattened. The eyes were wide apart, and the bridge of the nose was flat and broad. His lips were thin, and his ears were set low down on the sides of his head, almost meeting the jaw line. Although well nourished, he was underweight and his length and head size fell far below the normal standards for a six-month-old child.

Ruth and I returned to the respective sides of the lone desk in the office. "Do you know anything about his mother?" I asked, watching her cuddle Freddie in her arms as she tried to comfort him.

"No, that's all DCFS had," she responded.

"Well, with nothing more to go on, I can't really say anything for sure. But Freddie looks like a child whose mother used alcohol and drugs." It's always a hard sell to give this information to a foster mother, but Ruth had already made her own diagnosis, months ahead of me. "I know," was her only reply.

"There are some things we need to do." I outlined the various tests and procedures we would put Freddie through over the next several days. Ruth took in all the information in what I would learn was her usual style: gather the information, ask questions, make a decision. Patty came into the room to draw the blood work, Eilene scheduled the necessary tests at the hospital, and Ruth agreed to return in one week to get all the results.

The week went quickly. As Freddie's results started coming back into the office, I caught my breath, said a short prayer, and moved on.

Ruth appeared the next week, again garnering the first appointment in the morning, probably hoping to catch me at my freshest. "Ruth, the news isn't good." I was stumbling over my words, my voice hesitant. "Freddie's AIDS test is positive. At this young age, we don't know if it's positive because he actually caught AIDS from his mother or it's positive because he was just exposed and not infected. There's about a 30% chance he actually will have AIDS, but we won't know for sure until he's about 18 months old." The last words came out in a rush. I realized I'd been holding my breath.

Ruth sat quietly for a moment. "What'll we do?"

Foster and prospective adoptive parents face this kind of dilemma on a daily basis. Ruth never doubted that she would adopt Freddie, but these decisions don't always come easily. The most difficult part, of course, is looking into the future, trying to decide how much you are willing to accept as you consider adopting your child. To help understand what lies ahead for drug-exposed children, we will examine the impact of prenatal drug exposure through a developmental time frame, moving from the newborn period and early infancy to school age.

The newborn infant

Poor growth

The average birth weight of babies in the United States is 7 pounds 8 ounces, with a normal range down to about 5 pounds 8 ounces. In comparison, the average birth weight of drug-exposed infants is around 6 pounds 12 ounces, with a high percentage of the exposed newborns below 5 pounds 8 ounces. Such poor growth in the womb is one of the most common problems that occurs in substance-exposed newborns, especially if the mother smoked cigarettes in addition to using illegal drugs. Although as the child grows older, average weight usually "catches up" to normal, low birth weight is a significant risk factor for developmental outcome as the child gets older.

Often accompanying poor weight gain is poor head growth, a reflection of poor brain growth in the womb. The average head circumference at birth is about 35 cm (13 inches). A head circumference below about 33 cm at birth is small and an indication of risk. Alcohol, cocaine, and heroin have been shown to be the three drugs most closely associated with poor brain growth. In general small head circumference at birth is a significant marker of risk for poor developmental outcome. As drug-exposed children get older, head size usually does not reach the normal range until four to five years of age. For some prenatally exposed children, head size continues to be smaller throughout early childhood. A child with a medical history or noted evidence of small head size in proportion to body size should be a signal to examine the child's developmental history, which may help to explain some difficulties at home or in the classroom.

Prematurity

Drug- or alcohol-using women are more likely to smoke cigarettes, have infections complicating their pregnancy, and have inadequate prenatal care. In addition, cocaine and amphetamines have a direct effect on the uterus, causing contractions. Thus, it is not surprising that there is a high rate of prematurity (birth prior to 37 weeks gestation) among prenatally exposed infants. Premature delivery robs the fetus of the opportunity to reach full growth potential in the womb and places the child at increased risk for medical and developmental problems in the long term. Educationally, prematurity may show its effects in mild learning and behavioral problems. Again, however, because these children may live in a chaotic environment, it may be difficult to determine which effects are the result of prematurity, prenatal drug exposure, the environment, or a combination of all these factors.

Congenital malformations

Children who have been prenatally exposed to substances of abuse may suffer a range of physical problems, often based on the direct toxic effect of the substance (such as alcohol) or the interruption of adequate blood flow to developing organs caused by substances such as cocaine or amphetamines. Alcohol can produce structural changes in the face and head, while cocaine or amphetamine use during pregnancy can result in a baby's being born missing an arm, leg or fingers. In addition, babies exposed to cocaine or amphetamines prenatally have been reported to be missing a kidney or portions of the bowel due to infarction (death of the organ from lack of oxygen).

Central nervous system defects have been reported in babies whose mothers used cocaine or amphetamines during pregnancy. Small areas of infarction, or strokes, in the brain can occur throughout development or the baby can have a large stroke if the mother takes cocaine or amphetamines toward the end of pregnancy. Similar problems with the baby's having a heart attack while still in the womb also have been reported in infants whose mothers use cocaine or amphetamines.

Changes in muscle tone

Muscle tone is the strength and tension present in a baby's muscles. Alcohol exposure is associated with weak or poor muscle tone in the infant. Cocaine, amphetamines, phencyclidine (PCP, "angel dust"), and opiates such as heroin and methadone can produce tight, tremulous muscles in the exposed infant. This often is associated with arching behavior in which the infant arches his back when over stimulated and draws up his arms and legs, clenches his fists, and curls his toes. The infant also can have difficulty with feeding if muscle tone is affected, frequently chewing on the nipple without being able to coordinate suck and swallow.

Infectious diseases

The use of drugs and alcohol during pregnancy places the pregnant woman at high risk for a number of infections that can be passed to the fetus. From a broad perspective, any infection associated with blood borne transmission via dirty needles or any infection associated with exchange of body fluids, such as through sexual contact, occurs at increased frequency in substance abusing pregnant women. There are three major infections that must be considered in evaluating the infant placed in foster or adoptive care.

Syphilis – Syphilis is a sexually transmitted disease that can cause severe structural and neurological complications in the infant of an untreated mother. State laws require that all pregnant women be tested for syphilis. In addition, hospitals test all women at the time of delivery. Therefore, in most instances, it is easy for foster or adoptive parents to learn whether a woman had syphilis during pregnancy. If her test for syphilis was negative or if it was positive and she received adequate treatment with penicillin, the baby will not be affected. However, an untreated case of syphilis during pregnancy can cause severe complications in the newborn. If a mother has a positive syphilis test but was not treated for syphilis, her baby should be treated with a complete course of penicillin. This will protect the child and prevent any long-term complications.

HIV Infection – Acquired Immunodeficiency Syndrome (AIDS) is more prevalent among substance abusers than any other population. Passed through sharing needles as well as through sexual contact, every pregnant woman with a history of substance abuse should be tested for exposure to the Human Immunodeficiency Virus (HIV). If the woman is tested early in pregnancy and the test is negative, a repeat test is necessary in the third trimester if the woman has continued to use drugs or is sexually promiscuous. If a woman is negative for the HIV antibody in the third trimester, it is unlikely the child has been exposed to the AIDS virus and it is not necessary to test the infant, although some physicians and parents choose to do so.

If a pregnant HIV positive woman receives treatment during pregnancy with AZT, the child's chances of infection drop from about 30% down to about 10%. In any case, if a pregnant woman is positive for the HIV antibody, the newborn also will be positive. However, the positive test in the newborn may be due to the child's actual infection with HIV, or it may be due to passive passage of the mother's antibody across the placenta. There is no way of knowing the HIV positive newborn's status without conducting a PCR test or HIV culture on the baby. This test is available through most major medical centers and can differentiate true infection from passive antibody.

Hepatitis – Two major forms of hepatitis, B and C, occur more commonly in the drug using population. All pregnant women are tested for Hepatitis B during prenatal care or at the time of delivery, and all newborns should receive the first of a series of three vaccines against Hepatitis B before leaving the newborn nursery. This series of vaccines will protect the baby against acquiring Hepatitis B, even if the mother were infected. So in a practical sense, Hepatitis B is not usually a problem for foster or adoptive parents.

On the other hand, Hepatitis C is growing at epidemic rates in the United States, especially within the drug using population. Testing for Hepatitis C is not routine, but any newborn delivered to a substance-abusing woman should have a test for Hepatitis C prior to placement in a foster or adoptive home. If the baby is negative for Hepatitis C, there is no reason for further concern. However, if the baby is positive, he should have a PCR test to determine if he is truly infected (about a 5% chance) or if the positive antibody test is, as with AIDS, a result of passive transfer of the antibody from the mother. There is very little information about the long-term outcome of children born with Hepatitis C infection, but medical researchers are searching for treatment strategies. When exposure or infection is a concern, specific recommendations for testing and treatment can be found in the latest edition of the American Academy of Pediatrics' *Red Book*.

Special considerations for overseas adoptions – Institutionalization can cause depression, under-stimulation, and withdrawal in the child. Exacerbated by malnutrition, the immune system functions poorly, creating a high risk for contracting infectious diseases. In addition, there is an increasing number of children worldwide developing Acquired Immunodeficiency Syndrome (AIDS) due to widespread global drug trafficking, prostitution and sexually transmitted diseases in their mothers. Russia is a country poised for an epidemic of HIV reminiscent of the one experienced by the United States and Europe 15 years ago. Officials of the Russian Health Ministry reported 1500 new cases in 1996 and 100,000 in 1997. While the reported prevalence rate of children with HIV infection in countries from Asia and

Eastern Europe is not high, there have been occurrences of children who originally tested negative in their country of origin and were then found to be positive upon arrival in the United States.

Hepatitis B and C can be transmitted from the mother to the fetus, but transmission through contact with unsterile needles is increasing in orphanages across the world. Many countries do not have access to the Hepatitis B vaccine, particularly Asian countries where the prevalence rate is about 10% among children. In Romania, unscreened blood is used to treat malnourishment in children and thus increases the prevalence of HIV and Hepatitis B in the children. Evaluations of 65 children adopted from Romania between 1990 and 1991 found 20% were infected with Hepatitis B. Physicians from the United States tested 52 children residing in a Romanian orphanage in 1998 and found that 29% were infected with the disease.

The high prevalence of tuberculosis globally is well known, and children living in orphanages abroad are at especially high risk for contracting this disease due to poor medical care and improper nutrition. The long incubation period of tuberculosis can create the illusion of a well child until after arrival in the adopted country, and symptoms begin to present themselves at a later date. Data based on medical evaluations conducted in Boston, New York, and Minneapolis of internationally adopted children revealed that the prevalence rate of positive skin tests for TB in this population ranges between 3 and 17%.

Neurobehavioral changes
Newborn *neurobehavior* refers to the ability of infants to interact with their environment, to respond to stimulation, and to interact appropriately with the mother or other caretaker. Prenatal exposure to drugs may interfere with these capabilities. Although physical difficulties in prenatally exposed infants occur in only about 25% to 30% of cases, neurobehavioral deficiencies are far more common and are at the basis of the difficulties a parent may have in caring for the child.

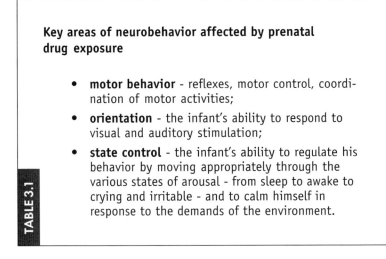

Key areas of neurobehavior affected by prenatal drug exposure

- **motor behavior** - reflexes, motor control, coordination of motor activities;
- **orientation** - the infant's ability to respond to visual and auditory stimulation;
- **state control** - the infant's ability to regulate his behavior by moving appropriately through the various states of arousal - from sleep to awake to crying and irritable - and to calm himself in response to the demands of the environment.

TABLE 3.1

Motor behavior – The *motor behaviors* of substance-exposed infants can vary widely. The infants may be quite stiff, with rigid posturing and hyperextension of the trunk. They may have difficulty reaching, grabbing, exploring objects, and bringing their hands to the midline, and their reflexes may be hyperactive. On the other hand, quite a few of these infants are very limp and lethargic at birth, with poor response to handling. In either case, the abnormal motor behavior interferes with coordination of the suck and swallow response, and feeding difficulties are not uncommon. Alcohol, cocaine, amphetamines, PCP, and heroin have all been shown to affect motor behaviors of newborn infants.

Orientation – *Orientation* capabilities suffer in newborns exposed to drugs prenatally, affecting the newborn's ability to respond to sound and to visual stimuli. Although the infant hears the sound, she has difficulty finding where the sound came from or showing attention to the sound. Visual stimuli have the same effect, with the child able to perceive that there is something to see but having difficulty focusing her gaze, even briefly, on the object. Children prenatally exposed to cocaine, heroin or PCP have difficulties with these orientation responses, and prenatal cocaine exposure particularly tends to interfere with visual orientation.

State control – *State control* refers to the way infants regulate their behavior as they respond to the environment around them. In substance-exposed infants, state control, or regulation, often is poorly organized, with the infants spending most of their time in states that shut them off from external stimulation. The infants frequently are very fragile, and their state changes tend to be abrupt and inappropriate with the child moving from sleeping to crying for no particular reason. In addition to the effects of heroin, cocaine, amphetamines, and PCP on state regulation, marijuana also can produce regulatory problems in the newborn and older child.

Four frequent patterns of state control problems in drug-exposed infants have been described:

- In the first pattern, the infants drop down into a deep self-protective sleep in response to the first stimulation received. These infants remain asleep and in fact enter a deeper sleep as attempts to awaken them increase, indicating they are protecting themselves from what they perceive as negative stimulation.

- The second pattern of state control demonstrated by drug-exposed infants is similar to the first except the infants cannot enter a sufficiently deep sleep to protect themselves from negative stimuli. They have difficulty blocking out negative stimuli, and rather than habituating or "getting use to," the stimuli, they remain asleep but continue to startle, whimper, change colors, breathe irregularly, and thrash around in response to stimulation.

- The third pattern of state control problems for drug-exposed infants is one in which they vacillate between sleeping and crying. With stimulation they break into agitated crying, and when the stimulation ceases they drop immediately back to a deep sleep. The continuous alternations between sleep and crying prevent the child from becoming sufficiently alert to respond adaptively to sound or to visual stimulation.

- The final and most common pattern of state control for drug-exposed infants is similar to the third in that these infants use both sleeping and crying to shut themselves off from over-stimulation. However, these infants, when managed carefully, are able to reach brief periods of alertness and can respond to the caretaker. The difficult aspect of this pattern is that the infants require intense but carefully regulated input. This generally requires a sophisticated degree of parenting that must be learned through foster and adoptive parent training.

In sum, the newborn with neurobehavioral difficulties can become easily overloaded and have difficulty regulating her behavior. Sudden change in light or sound levels can disrupt sleep. The infant demonstrates frequent startles and color changes as she becomes over-stimulated, and rapid changes in level of responsiveness can confuse the parent and disrupt interactions between the infant and the parent. It is important to remember that the behaviors the infant is demonstrating are not a rejection of the parent but rather biologically based and must be understood in this context.

Intervention Strategies for the Newborn Infant

The best intervention strategy for the newborn with neurobehavioral problems focuses on meeting the needs of the child and adjusting interactions with her based on what she can tolerate. If the baby begins changing colors, sneezing, or hiccoughing, this usually is a signal that the child is getting overloaded. The parent should step back, and give her some "cool down" time. A pacifier can help calm the infant. If the baby's behavior begins to escalate, swaddling her in a blanket will help her gain control. General guidelines for helping your infant include:

- Don't let your baby get over-upset and frantic.

  Watch for early signs that the baby is getting upset: yawning, sneezing, hiccuping, jitteriness, skin color changes, refusing to look at you.

- If your baby keeps crying and isn't able to stop, quietly and gently soothe her by wrapping her snugly in a light blanket, giving her a pacifier, and rocking back and forth. Sometimes it helps to have the baby face away from you.

- Be careful to calm your baby in ways that she can tolerate.

  Babies need stimulation. When the baby is awake and calm you can work on getting her use to your face and voice by smiling, making eye contact, and talking softly. But just use one kind of stimulation at a time.

- As she gets use to you, increase the amount of stimulation you give your baby.

  Talk, sing, smile, rock or move your baby's arms and legs very gently. Her cues will tell you what she likes or doesn't like. When the baby is calm, unwrap her to allow her to move her arms and legs freely. Wrap her up again if she starts showing any signs of distress.

TABLE 3.2

Through the first year of life, prenatally exposed infants may demonstrate early signs of difficulty with regulating and controlling their behavior. By six months of age, the drug-exposed infant often is described as restless and difficult to comfort. By one year of age, he is easily overloaded and cannot tolerate too much stimulation at once. For example, a one-year-old infant, if given a cube and a cup, will place the cube into the cup. When presented with eight cubes, a one-year-old will place at least three of the cubes into the cup. On the other hand, a one-year-old drug-exposed child, although able to put one cube into a cup if presented with one cube and a cup, will become agitated if presented with a cup and eight cubes at once. The child frequently will turn pale, begin looking around the room, become increasingly agitated, and then scoop the cubes off the table. This phenomenon of easy overload is an important indicator of a regulatory problem, and parents must learn to provide stimulation slowly and in measured doses in order not to overload the child.

A study of three-month-old infants who had been prenatally exposed to cocaine found the children's cognitive development was normal. However, arousal and attention regulation were affected, and the infants had difficulty responding appropriately to various stimuli. As a component of this difficulty, the children continue to demonstrate poor habituation; that is, they are unable to screen out negative stimuli and are easily distracted by them. It is not unusual for parents to note that their drug-exposed child is always the first individual to hear an airplane overhead or a bus driving by the outside window.

This distractibility can interfere with the child's play patterns. Researchers from the University of California at Los Angeles found that a group of 18 month-old children who had been exposed in the womb to cocaine showed striking deficits in the stability and organization of free play. They had less pretend play than comparison children. The majority of drug-exposed children demonstrated a high rate of scattering, batting, and picking up and putting down toys rather than sustained combining of toys, fantasy play, or curious exploration. This pattern of disruptive and disorganized play appears to be similar to the problems with neurobehavioral regulation as described in newborns affected by prenatal drug exposure. Parents of drug-exposed infants often report that it is difficult to get the child to sit on the parent's lap and look at a book because other objects or activities in the room easily distract the child.

The preschool-age child

Although we now have a growing body of research on the effects of perinatal substance abuse on the newborn and young infant, until relatively recently little attention had been paid to the long-term implications of a mother's drug use during pregnancy. Drawing firm conclusions from many of these studies is difficult because it is hard to distinguish the purely biological effects of the prenatal exposure from the on-going environmental problems caused by living in a home with a substance-abusing parent.

A research team from Seattle, Washington, evaluated the effects of prenatal exposure to alcohol on IQ scores at four years of age. They found a significant relationship between alcohol consumption during pregnancy and low IQ scores of the women's four-year-old children. Research also is documenting that tobacco smoking by the pregnant woman is related to poor language development and cognitive functioning in the three and four-year-old child. In addition, prenatal marijuana exposure can result in poor verbal and memory capabilities in the four-year-old child.

Studies consistently report that prenatal exposure to cocaine, heroin, and other illegal drugs has minimal direct influence on intellectual development in children through three years of age, but is one of many factors that influences intellectual abilities. Most specifically, it is becoming increasingly clear that, after genetics, the single most important predictor of cognitive development is the environment in which the child is being raised. This has tremendous implications for the adopted child and is good news for most prospective adoptive parents. However, it also should be noted that although intellectual development can be normal, adopted drug-exposed children demonstrate significant behavioral difficulties that can interfere with their developmental progress.

■   Sara is an example of a drug- and alcohol-exposed child who had significant behavioral problems related to her difficulty in processing information and regulating her behavior.

At two years of age, Sara's foster mother and a DCFS caseworker brought her to the Child Study Center for an evaluation to determine if Sara should stay in foster care or be returned to her biological father.   In fact, Sara had been receiving Spanish tutoring in preparation for return to her father.

Sara had been a healthy newborn, weighing 7 pounds 8 ounces. Her mother had a history of heavy alcohol use and had used cocaine at least once a month during pregnancy.   At birth, Sara's urine was positive for cocaine and marijuana.   She went home at three days of age to her foster family.   Things seemed to go well at first, but by 18 months of age, her behaviors were becoming more and more difficult for her foster parents to handle.   In fact, Sara's day care center had already asked her to leave because she had been hitting and biting other children.

Sara's foster mother reports that in addition to the aggressive behavior seen in day care, Sara eats dirt, toilet paper, cat food, or other non-food material at home.   She shows remarkably little response to painful stimuli, and her foster mother has seen her touch a hot frying pan without flinching.   Visits with her biological father precipitate more clingy behavior, and her appetite is disrupted.   Sara's sleep, in general, also is a problem.   She usually falls asleep easily within ten minutes, but wakens frequently, usually in response to noises.   Unfortunately the family lives near a train track, and Sara is exhibiting more and more sensitivity to the sound of the train's whistle, both waking and whimpering at night as well as startling and crying in the daytime.   Naps are infrequent and last less than thirty minutes.   At night, Sara requires a small blanket over head and the foster mother's applying deep pressure to her back in order to fall asleep.

There have been frequent instances of Sara's putting herself in danger by going with strangers or disobeying her foster mother's clear instructions. Sara has been told many times not to run into the street. However, just the week before the visit, Sara had been running toward the street. Her foster mother yelled out that there was a truck coming. Sara turned, saw the truck, agreed that it was indeed coming, but ran out into the street anyway. The truck driver's quick stop averted a tragedy.

At the Child Study Center, it was immediately noted that Sara was very difficult to control unless she was held in her foster mother's arms. When placed on the floor, she became very active, distractible, and impulsive. Although very mobile, she was clumsy, seeming not to be planning her next move.

On physical examination, Sara was very small, especially her head size. Her mid-face was flattened, and her facial features were those of a child who had been exposed to alcohol during pregnancy. The rest of her physical exam was normal except for mild weakness in her trunk and lower extremities.

Sara's play was very disorganized, and she scattered and dumped toys, at one point throwing a block at the child psychologist. The child had one tantrum during the evaluation, which the foster mother ignored. Sara had great difficulty with self-regulation, demonstrating low frustration tolerance, distractibility, limited attention, and easy over-stimulation. She did not respond well to tactile stimulation, being very defensive when touched. On formal developmental testing, Sara scored in the low normal range on mental score and well within normal for motor scores.

Many of Sara's behaviors are those seen in drug-exposed children. Although overall development is normal, her impulsiveness, short attention span, high activity level and ease of over-stimulation interfere with successful task completion, learning, and social development. Drug-exposed children also frequently exhibit difficulties in regulating their affect and are indiscriminate socially, knowing no boundaries in their interactions with strangers.

Cognitive development is impeded by poor concept formation, and a drug-exposed toddler often will have difficulty understanding the difference, for example, when told to put a block under the table or over the table. The parent often mistakenly identifies impaired memory and retention of information as noncompliance rather than understanding that this is a competency issue. In addition, Sara, as do many of the children, demonstrates her organizational deficits through her scattering of toys and her lack of meaningful engagement with the toys.

Sara could not process information; thus, cause and effect had little meaning for her. She saw the truck coming, but that fact had no impact on her impulsive decision to run into the street. Finally, we know that young children learn through their sensory world. Children with an inability to process information from their senses in a meaningful and productive way seek sensory stimulation in any way they can find it. In Sara's case, hitting and biting other children was not a matter of aggression; she was seeking sensory input that she could understand and use.

▮ ▮

The early school-age child

Advances in understanding the school-age child who was exposed to drugs and alcohol prenatally have come slowly, but over the last few years, consistent patterns of development and behavior have been recognized. In a longitudinal controlled study of children exposed to cocaine, alcohol and other drugs during gestation, it was found that by six years of age, 60% of the children's birth mothers were continuing to use drugs and alcohol. In addition, children in homes in which there was ongoing substance abuse were much more likely to have been exposed to violence: to have lost a close relative to a violent death, to have been exposed to domestic violence within the home, to have a mother who had been sexually abused or raped, and to have a mother who had previously physically abused a child. Given these issues, it was not surprising to find that the most important factor predicting the child's IQ at six years of age was the mother's drug use patterns in the six years after delivery rather than her drug use patterns during pregnancy. A home in which drugs were being used was a home in which the child's needs for stimulation and developmental support were not being met.

On the other hand, children prenatally exposed to drugs and alcohol at six years of age demonstrated consistent behavioral difficulties unrelated to their mothers' drug use patterns following delivery. School aged drug- and alcohol-exposed children, whether living in their biologic home or in an adoptive home, demonstrated significantly higher levels of:

- *anxiety/depression:* feels need to be perfect; feels unloved; feels others out to get him; feels worthless or inferior; nervous/high strung/tense; sad/unhappy; worries; nervous/anxious

- *social problems:* acts too young for age; clingy; doesn't get along with others; gets teased a lot; not liked by other kids.

- *thought problems:* can't get mind off certain thoughts; repeats certain acts over and over; stares; strange ideas; strange behavior.

- *attention problems:* can't concentrate for long; can't sit still/restless; confused; daydreams; impulsive; poor schoolwork; stares.

- *delinquent behavior:* no guilt after misbehaving; lies/cheats; prefers older kids; steals; hangs around with kids who get into trouble.

- *aggressive behavior:* argues a lot; demands attention; destroys things of his own or others; disobedient at home and/or school; stubborn; sudden changes in mood; talks too much; unusually loud; temper tantrums/hot temper.

These difficulties can be understood more easily if they are divided into two types of behavior: *over-controlled* and *under-controlled*. In clinical practice, we refer to the child who is expending much of his energy controlling feelings and inhibiting his own behavior, especially repressing anger or other negative feelings toward others, as being "over-controlled." This term describes the energy expended in the service of these behaviors. Children who are over-controlled typically show patterns of withdrawal, anxiety, social isolation, and depression. Drug-exposed children with high levels of anxiety are easily frustrated when presented with challenging situations, feel others are out to get them, and can feel unloved, worthless or inferior. The newborn infant who averted his gaze and withdrew into a deep sleep when over stimulated has become the little boy who wanders around the classroom without fully engaging in any activity, who gives up easily, or becomes upset when encountering any difficulty. These children are generally insecure and question their own capabilities, blaming themselves for their shortcomings.

Children with "under-controlled" behaviors have difficulty controlling or inhibiting their behavior, demonstrating impulsivity, aggression, and over activity in the classroom or family setting. Prenatally exposed children exhibiting these patterns are often characterized as "hyperactive." This reflects the children's low threshold for stimulation and difficulty regulating themselves, especially when frustrated. The baby girl who could not easily move from a crying state to a calm interactive state can be seen as the preschooler who cannot calm down after recess or becomes out of control when she is not allowed to do what she wants.

The picture of the drug-exposed child that emerges from research is one in which the child:

- is poorly organized,
- has trouble regulating her behavior,
- has trouble staying on track and completing a task,
- has higher activity levels, has low frustration levels and poor tolerance for stimulation (i.e., easily over stimulated),
- experiences more anxiety and depression.

The range and severity of behavioral difficulties is, of course, wide, and there simply is no way to identify the child who was prenatally exposed to drugs simply on the basis of behavior. However, several studies indicate a significant relationship between prenatal drug exposure and behavior. In addition, recent studies have found that frequent custody changes and violence in the biologic home make the problem behaviors worse. Thus, we must be sure to view the exposed child as he should be viewed, not as willfully disobedient, but as a child whose neurological system may have been affected by the drugs that crossed the placenta during pregnancy.

── **CASE STUDY: Anthony**

▌ Anthony illustrates the multiple behavioral and learning difficulties that can emerge in the drug-exposed child.

Anthony is an almost seven-year-old child who was brought to the Child Study Center by his foster parents. The parents have been planning to adopt Anthony, but now are hesitant because of his increasing behavioral difficulties.

Anthony was born at full term to a mother who received no prenatal care and reportedly used alcohol and cocaine throughout pregnancy. Anthony's birth weight was 4 pounds 6 ounces, his birth length was 17 ½ inches and his birth head circumference was 29 ½ cm. While in the hospital, his mother's urine toxicology screen was positive for cocaine.

Anthony lived with his biological family until age three years, then lived in four consecutive foster placements. At the age of five years eight months, he and his siblings (now ages 11 years and 8 years) were placed in the current foster home with a goal of adoption. The family was advised that Anthony and his siblings were healthy and free of special needs or significant risk factors. They were devastated when the children began to display social, emotional, behavioral, and developmental delays. After Anthony's older brother was diagnosed with Fetal Alcohol Syndrome (FAS), the parents initiated evaluations for each child.

Anthony's foster parents' main concerns regard his emotional, behavioral, developmental, and learning difficulties. The foster parents describe Anthony as being defiant and aggressively cruel to others and to animals. They state that Anthony lacks remorse and has little regard for others' needs and feelings. Anthony also has difficulty learning and abiding by basic safety and home rules. Consequently, the foster parents are concerned that his behavior places the other children in their home at risk for harm and abuse.

The parents describe Anthony as inattentive and unable to tolerate frustration. In the past he has made some attempt to learn rules and family expectations, but such efforts have deteriorated over the past several months. The parents also describe Anthony as emotionally defensive and distant, a boy who refused to cry or show vulnerability for months after his arrival in their home. Finally, they are concerned about his ability to learn (e.g., hasn't mastered concept of "yesterday, today, tomorrow") and to achieve academic and social success in school. Teachers have described Anthony as frequently hyperactive and unable to focus on the task at hand. He has difficulty playing and getting along with his peers. The school has refused to provide special educational services, nor will they conduct an evaluation.

Anthony wets the bed nightly and frequently does not hold his urine during the day, not seeming to be troubled by his accidents. It takes Anthony quite a while to fall asleep at night – he likes to chat and stay awake after going to bed. About 1 ½ hours after falling asleep, Anthony falls out of the bed, but then goes back to sleep easily.

During the evaluation at the Child Study Center, Anthony was cheerful and verbal, initiating conversation and engaging the examiner. At the outset of testing, Anthony was very cooperative and attentive. He put forth great effort, even on difficult items and attempted to sound out words and to make intelligent guesses on items beyond his skill level. He took pride in performing well and had difficulty saying, "I don't know," even on items beyond his level. After a short break, he displayed hyperactivity (squirming in chair, difficulty remaining seated, wanting to end the testing and leaving the room) and inattention (needing frequent redirection to the question at hand). His level of cooperation waned and he repeatedly complained of wanting to leave. His mood remained stable, with appropriate range of affect. His speech was clear; thoughts were logical and goal-directed. He displayed no comprehension problems or apparent memory deficits. No psychotic symptoms or suicidal thoughts were evident during the testing.

Results of Anthony's evaluation indicated that Anthony had developed stronger verbal than non-verbal problem-solving abilities. His Verbal IQ score was in the Average range, while his Performance IQ score fell at the low end of the Low Average range. This score difference prevented an accurate assessment of his overall (Full Scale IQ) cognitive functioning. A relative verbal strength did emerge, which suggested strong intellectual curiosity and a positive attitude toward school and learning. However, Anthony's below-average visual-motor speed, coordination, and organization, as documented on testing, as well as his high distractibility, represented impediments to classroom performance. Additionally, below average reading and arithmetic scores indicated current learning problems.

Non-verbal weaknesses also emerged in visual concentration and alertness to environmental details; thus, he may seem quite oblivious to environmental feedback and social cues. This finding was supported by Sensory Profile results, which suggested Anthony has difficulty processing sensory input. This impairs accurate reception and processing of sensory information, as well as formulation of appropriate and adaptive responses to that input. Thus, his responses to social and environmental situations may seem quite ineffective or inappropriate at times.

Anthony's visual memory scores were inconsistent. On a measure of memory for abstract designs, he scored significantly below average; however, his memory for objects within a meaningful context fell at the high end of the average range. His verbal memory scores were more consistent, indicating intact rote learning abilities, with average (but lower) ability to remember more complex verbal material. His inconsistent delayed recall performance likely reflected difficulty retrieving stored information.

Anthony demonstrated significant ambivalence regarding contact with others and with his environment, making him seem aloof or emotionally inaccessible. This uncomfortable conflict (ambivalence) may have contributed to impulsive acting out and aggressive behavior when he became emotionally overwhelmed and threatened. Anthony had fundamental doubt of others' intentions to provide care and nurturance. This was most likely due to his early experiences of neglect and abuse. As a result, he felt lonely, isolated, and had difficulty accepting the love and caring that was provided. He was a boy struggling with overwhelmingly sad and helpless feelings.

Anthony met criteria for a diagnosis of ADHD, Combined Type, based on his poor concentration, impulsivity, poor school performance, and fidgeting. A diagnosis of Oppositional Defiant Disorder (argues; disobedient) needed to be ruled out through further clinical assessment. Likewise, a diagnosis of Reactive Attachment Disorder, Inhibited Type (inappropriate social interactions) must also be confirmed or ruled out based on further clinical evaluation. Potential learning problems should be monitored and confirmed by classroom observation and psychoeducational testing by the school.

Problems with emotional and behavioral regulation, learning, and attachment are frequently found in children with prenatal drug exposure. However, it is important to note that Anthony had many strengths that could serve as protective factors that would promote positive development. Anthony was described as a child who enjoyed coloring, drumming and who liked to take care of family members. He could be kind, helpful, and fun to play with. Anthony was quite capable of learning, although he required alternative teaching strategies that were more conducive to his skills and abilities. These strengths would likely enhance his efforts to manage difficulties in the future.

Based on the results of this evaluation, several recommendations were made that could help Anthony succeed:

1. Anthony's school must closely monitor his classroom performance in order to identify his behavioral and emotional needs in the classroom, as well as to monitor for the emergence of learning disorders.

The school should review the results of this evaluation to determine the need for additional psychoeducational testing to address his needs and provide services that will ensure his support and success in the educational environment.

2. Classroom techniques to promote positive behavior should be instituted:

- frequent rewards and reinforcement for positive on-task behavior;
- keep written and verbal information simple;
- underline key words and directions;
- create brief lessons and short assignments;
- communicate clearly using brief, precise directions, repeated directions;
- have the child repeat directions to ensure his understanding;
- provide feedback about his performance and allow opportunities for self-correction.

3. Parents and teachers should utilize educational strategies that minimize distraction (seating away from windows, noisy places, distracting peers) and maximize positive models (seat near teacher/ parent or model peers, use frequent eye contact).

4. Anthony will benefit from his teacher's modeling and teaching a five-step problem-solving approach: A) What is the problem? B) What are my options/solutions? C) Which is the best solution to use? D) Apply the solution E) Evaluate results. If successful give positive feedback; if not, return to Step B.

5. Occupational therapy (OT) can address Anthony's sensory integration deficits, which affect all areas of his functioning. Additionally, an adaptive behavior assessment should be administered to evaluate current daily living, communication, and socialization skill levels. Delays in these areas also can be addressed through occupational therapy services.

6. Individual psychotherapy is recommended to address emotional issues related to early neglect, possible abuse, and multiple place-

ments. Play therapy is recommended to help Anthony access and process these themes in a non-threatening, age-appropriate manner. Therapy techniques to enhance positive coping skills, self-esteem, emotional expression skills, and social problem-solving skills should be emphasized. A supportive, therapeutic relationship can also help Anthony establish trust and the acceptance of love, nurturance, and caring.

7. The foster parents should enroll in a behavioral parent training component of the therapy. They require training in how to help Anthony develop trust, self-regulation, and positive coping skills. The training also will support the parents' efforts to understand his limitations and to cope more positively with challenging emotional, behavioral, and learning needs.

8. Considering developmental challenges and special needs, respite care should be provided to allow the foster parents to renew their energy, resources, and resolve to continue providing a consistent, loving, structured home for Anthony.

9. Anthony should participate in appropriate social and sports activities in order to work on behavioral and emotional control, social competence and acceptance. The parents may contact the local Park District regarding Special Recreation activities in the area.

10. Anthony's social, emotional, and behavioral deficits place him at higher risk for potential injury and abuse. He requires close monitoring by adults in all settings to help him make safe, positive decisions and resolve confusion or conflicts in a sensible manner. All caregivers and educators must be alerted to neurodevelopmental limitations related to suspected prenatal substance exposure.

In the one year following implementation of these recommendations, Anthony's behavior and school achievement did improve. However, medication management was required to help supplement the interventions and to help Anthony focus on his tasks. He still has not been adopted.

■ ■

Implications for adolescence

Numerous researchers have found that psychological character-istics identified as early as age six can foretell the child's drug use a decade later. Studies have defined such early characteristics as:

- the inability to get along well with other children or a lack of social competence;
- poor impulse control;
- inattention and inability to concentrate;
- a general sense of emotional distress or liability.

Unfortunately, these are the very characteristics one often sees in the drug-exposed child. For children from substance abusing fami-lies, impaired parenting only serves to enhance the risk, fostering childhood behaviors that are characteristic of adolescent drug abus-ers. Thus, foster and adoptive parents must recognize that in addi-tion to heightened susceptibility for alcoholism in later life from a genetic perspective, the hyperactivity, conduct disorder, oppositional behavior and delinquency the children display during childhood and adolescence put them at even greater risk for substance abuse. As an adopted or foster child approaches preadolescence, her impulsive behavior will place her at great risk for experimentation with drugs and alcohol. Therefore, it is important that parents explain to the child her biologic inclination for addiction and the need to avoid experimentation, a not unusual component of adolescence.

Freddie is 14 years old now. He has AIDS, but his AIDS doesn't define him. He has a colostomy, takes a combination of six different drugs every day, and is on the ninth grade basketball team. When the other school parents tried to prevent Freddie from joining the team, his teammates protested and re-fused to play unless Freddie was allowed on the team. He plays guard.

4

Understanding Children's Behavior

To understand children's behavioral problems, it is important to have a perspective on behavior at different ages. In general, as children become older, their behavior becomes more focused and specific, with increasing self-control and responsibility. For instance, the mainly exploratory behavior of toddlers gradually gives way to behavior that is purposeful and organized, showing the beginning of industriousness and initiative by the time of school entry.

A behavior that may be considered normal at one age can be a problem at another age. A good example is separation anxiety. In the first and second years of life, it is very normal for children to show anxiety and fear about being separated from their parents or primary caregivers. As children get older, this anxiety typically decreases to where the behavior occurs only in specific situations. Many children become upset about leaving the parent on the first day of kindergarten. Normally, this anxiety subsides as the child becomes comfortable in the new surroundings. If the behavior continues throughout the primary grades, it indicates that the child is experiencing significant difficulties and warrants a professional consultation.

Trajectories

Development is often conceptualized as occurring along trajectories, or pathways. A child's development occurs along multiple trajectories simultaneously, with each trajectory signifying a different domain or area of development, including cognitive, emotional, social, interpersonal, and motor. A child may be on a healthy trajectory in one or more domains but be on a less than optimal trajectory in another domain. These trajectories are assumed to be linear and continuous, unless something occurs to redirect the pathway. Thus, the goal for those of us who work with children is to affect the trajectory in a positive way, so that the less optimal pathways are impeded and the long-term trajectory of a given child is modified in the appropriate and healthy direction.

"Just being a kid"

When behavioral problems occur, there may be a tendency to forget that, at times, the child is "just being a kid." The parent or teacher should not assume every inappropriate behavior or series of behaviors indicates the presence of a problem. Often, even the child who has been identified as having behavioral problems simply may be exhibiting behavior typical of other children of the same age. All children may show at different times, depending on the circumstances and the child's characteristics, a degree of inattention, distractibility, withdrawal, aggressiveness, mild disobedience, and being off task.

Beyond "normal": When behaviors become problems

Those who live and work with children often ask how to know when a behavior is "abnormal" or problematic versus when it is merely a manifestation of a wide range of "normal." Among the criteria for making this determination are frequency of the behavior, duration of the problem, whether the behavior is having a detrimental impact on the child's learning, and whether the child's relationships with peers or adults are negatively affected.

Frequency

"Frequency" refers to how often a behavior occurs and whether it occurs often enough to impact a child's success in one of the domains of development. Examples include how often the child fails to complete assignments, number of times a student engages in off-task behavior, or the frequency of the child's talking without permission. An important question to ask is, "Do such behaviors occur with such frequency that they interfere with healthy learning or relationships?"

Duration

How long a behavior persists is referred to as duration. If an undesired or inappropriate behavior persists for so long that the child's performance is affected, then the behavior is problematic. Examples include how long a child remains off task or how pervasively a child withdraws from social situations.

In most cases, assessing both frequency and duration is an important first step in determining if there is a deleterious effect on the child's successful development. For example, the child may be off task for several minutes at a time (duration), while making distracting noises or getting out of his chair several times during the same period (frequency). It may be necessary to consider both the time off task as well as the frequency of other negative behaviors that occur during that time. However, the most important consideration is whether the behavior is having an adverse impact on the child's learning, social relationships with peers, and interactions with adults.

Problems in behavioral regulation

Impulsive, inattentive, and overactive behavior is the major problem seen in children who were exposed to alcohol or illegal drugs in the womb. Not only do the children disrupt the home and classroom, but they also may have difficulty learning and achieving. These behaviors are characteristic of children who have a problem in regulating their behavior, the most common chronic behavior disorder, the most common single source of referrals to child mental health centers, and one of the most common difficulties confronting parents and teachers.

Children with problems in behavioral regulation demonstrate inappropriate responses to environmental stimuli, particularly a lack of behavioral inhibition. These problems are manifest at home and in the classroom as poor attention to tasks, impulsive behavior, organizational difficulties, distractibility, and over-activity. Children with such problems are enigmatic to their parents and teachers, and their unpredictable behavior often leads to the erroneous belief that their behaviors reflect a lack of motivation or desire to do well rather than a biologically based disability.

The underlying cause of behavioral regulation difficulties is not completely clear. We do know, however, that neurological, physiological, genetic, environmental, toxic, and psychosocial factors have all been correlated with behavior regulation problems. In a study of 22,000 children from a general population of American children, 18.7% had behavioral difficulties, and about half of these, or 9.2% of the total sample, showed evidence of attentional or hyperactivity problems that interfered with learning. Within this group, the children with pervasive, disorganized high reactivity and extremely short attention spans, about 1% to 2%, were easily recognizable as "hyperactive" and were receiving behavioral interventions and medication for their problems. However, the other 5% to 10% of the children did not demonstrate behavior problems but did have difficulties with attention and regulation that significantly interfered with their learning and participation in the classroom environment.

The biologic basis of behavior

Biochemical research has begun to gather evidence of possible linkages between prenatal exposure to drugs and behavioral regulation problems. For example, cocaine blocks the way neurotransmitters such as serotonin, dopamine, and norepinephrine are stored in the brain. Cocaine produces a "high" by increasing the availability of these transmitters at the nerve ends and increasing the excitation of the nerves. Over a period of chronic exposure, a dampening effect may be produced, and the number of dopamine receptors available at the nerve ending diminishes. PET scans of adults with a long history of cocaine use have shown an absence of functioning dopamine receptors in the prefrontal cortex. This is the section of the brain that controls impulsive and aggressive behavior. Thus, these types of studies help us understand the behavioral regulation problems that we see in children who are exposed to drugs during pregnancy.

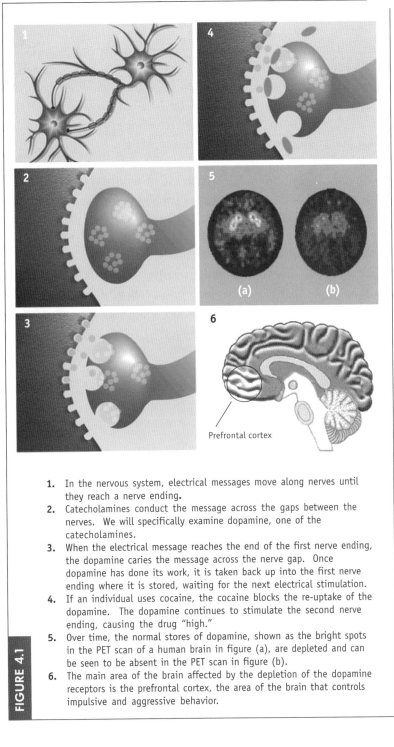

1. In the nervous system, electrical messages move along nerves until they reach a nerve ending.
2. Catecholamines conduct the message across the gaps between the nerves. We will specifically examine dopamine, one of the catecholamines.
3. When the electrical message reaches the end of the first nerve ending, the dopamine caries the message across the nerve gap. Once dopamine has done its work, it is taken back up into the first nerve ending where it is stored, waiting for the next electrical stimulation.
4. If an individual uses cocaine, the cocaine blocks the re-uptake of the dopamine. The dopamine continues to stimulate the second nerve ending, causing the drug "high."
5. Over time, the normal stores of dopamine, shown as the bright spots in the PET scan of a human brain in figure (a), are depleted and can be seen to be absent in the PET scan in figure (b).
6. The main area of the brain affected by the depletion of the dopamine receptors is the prefrontal cortex, the area of the brain that controls impulsive and aggressive behavior.

FIGURE 4.1

ADHD

Parents often ask whether the behavioral problems their child is exhibiting are due to prenatal drug exposure or Attention Deficit Hyperactivity Disorder (ADHD). Because the neurochemical basis of both conditions is so similar, we prefer to view both groups of children as having problems in behavioral regulation rather than focusing on trying to differentiate behavioral problems due to substance exposure from difficulties due to ADHD.

Overall, Attention Deficit Hyperactivity Disorder (ADHD) occurs in 6% to 9% of children, with onset usually before age seven. The recognition and diagnosis of ADHD depends on observations of parents and teachers. The hallmark symptoms are inattention, impulsive behavior, and over-activity in two or more settings. However, recent research views the inability to inhibit behavior as the overriding difficulty in ADHD; that is, attention problems, impulsive behavior, and high levels of developmentally inappropriate behavior are the result of the child's having difficulties in regulating and inhibiting behavior. Although no direct correlation between intellectual development and behavior regulation problems has been documented, children with ADHD have significantly higher rates of impaired academic adjustment, grade failure, placement in special education, and lower levels of academic achievement.

There is no consensus as to the cause of ADHD, but multiple factors, including genetic, environmental, and toxic, appear to come together to produce the symptomatic behaviors. Recent animal research has documented that changes in the brain's stores of catecholamines, especially dopamine, result in self-regulatory problems that can interfere with the maturing executive functioning of the child. Such functioning, including planning, implementing, and evaluating, is essential for learning and intellectual development. Executive functioning relies on connections between the dopamine structures and the brain's frontal lobes.

Given the plausible common neurological basis of ADHD and prenatal drug exposure, it is not surprising that it may be difficult to differentiate the behaviors of children with known prenatal exposure from children who are diagnosed with ADHD. The common physiology and behavioral symptoms of children with features of ADHD and those with prenatal drug exposure provides a theoretical foundation from which to develop common interventions for a broad range of children with problems in behavioral regulation.

A systematic approach to children's behavioral problems

As we consider the problem of regulatory difficulties in children with prenatal drug exposure, it is helpful to have a systematic understanding of children's behavioral problems. When you observe your child, you may be able to identify a pattern of the behaviors: aggressiveness, withdrawal, unhappiness, or anxiety, to name a few. However, many times the behaviors do not appear to have a pattern or to be caused by identifiable events. For example, a child may suddenly become aggressive for no apparent reason, causing confusion and uncertainty for the parent as to how to intervene. In this case, viewing the child's behavior systematically can guide the development of effective interventions for the child.

Over-controlled behavior

Over-controlled behavior refers to those regulatory patterns in which children expend a great deal of energy controlling their feelings and inhibiting their behavior. Such children often show patterns of withdrawal and social isolation and may be difficult to identify because they usually are not disruptive. They often sit in the back of the classroom and are perceived as being shy, compliant and reluctant to engage in activities. Up to ten percent of all children have these kinds of problems, but they are identified in fewer than half the cases.

Over-controlled behaviors are sometimes also referred to as "internalizing patterns." The child's feelings are directed inwardly or "internally" so that the child experiences depression, anxiety or low self-esteem and lacks self-confidence and self-efficacy. The parent and classroom teacher should be alert to indications of these patterns, as children who have been exposed to alcohol, cocaine and other drugs and who live in stressful environments are more likely to demonstrate them.

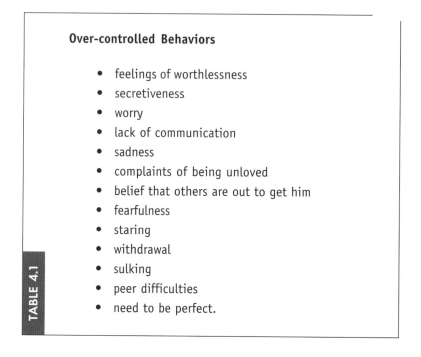

TABLE 4.1

Over-controlled Behaviors

- feelings of worthlessness
- secretiveness
- worry
- lack of communication
- sadness
- complaints of being unloved
- belief that others are out to get him
- fearfulness
- staring
- withdrawal
- sulking
- peer difficulties
- need to be perfect.

CASE STUDY: Susie -- excessive talking

Susie is talking in class without permission, and the teacher reprimands her. Susie becomes very quiet for the next hour. However, observing her on the playground during recess, Susie interacts well and shows no signs of withdrawal. Back in the classroom, she behaves appropriately and responds well to directions and completes tasks.

Case discussion

Since past observations of Susie's behavior suggest that usually she is well behaved, her brief withdrawal behavior in response to the reprimand is situation-specific and should not be considered an internalizing, or over-controlled, pattern of behavior. All children, at times, will talk out of turn, like Susie (i.e., "just being a kid") so it is not a serious problem that warrants specific interventions.

Compare this scenario to Sammy.

CASE STUDY: Sammy -- withdrawn behavior

Sammy does not seem to enjoy working with other children, but rather spends much of his time alone, both in and out of the classroom, and rarely smiles. He has a need for everything to be perfect, and lack of perfection seems to confirm his feelings of inadequacy. He rarely participates in classroom activities or volunteers answers, and he seems very tense and uncomfortable when called upon to participate, often lowering his eyes and not responding. When he does respond he frequently speaks so softly he cannot be heard.

Case discussion

Although much more information would be needed in an actual case, the withdrawal shown here is part of a chronic pattern that is presumed to be interfering with Sammy's schoolwork. Drug-exposed children have a low tolerance for frustration and often attempt to withdraw from typical classroom situations. Fear and insecurity often prompt their behavior.

Children who live in environments in which drugs are being used often do not have effective conversational skills because their parents have failed to respond positively to their verbal initiations, resulting in a lack of experience with verbal interaction and expression. They have difficulty with internal emotional language so that they cannot express their feelings. These children also may have difficulty reading social and emotional cues. All this leads to high levels of social anxiety, and the children often lapse into daydreaming as an escape from such anxieties. If the foster or adoptive parent or teacher suspects this is the case, referral may be indicated and collaboration with other professionals may be needed as well. However, the parents are in a primary position to help the child with these difficult feelings and to develop strategies to improve his social functioning.

The essential difference between Susie and Sammy is Susie's behavior is in direct response to a specific situation and is not a chronic pattern, while Sammy has exhibited a long-term pattern of dysfunction that seems to bridge different situations and conditions.

Under-controlled behavior

Under-controlled behavior patterns are more easily identified in children because the behaviors tend to be disruptive. "Acting out" is one way that these types of behaviors often are labeled. Whereas children with over-controlled or internalizing behavior tend to inhibit behavior, turning their feelings inward, the under-controlled (also termed "externalizing") child has much difficulty in inhibiting or controlling behavior and expresses his feelings outwardly, usually against others.

There are two categories of behaviors within the larger grouping of under-controlled behavior. Children with a conduct disorder or oppositional-defiant disorder fall into one category because they have difficulty managing aggression and anger. Another category of children is those who meet criteria for Attention Deficit Disorder or Attention Deficit Hyperactivity Disorder. These children have difficulty with sustained attention to task and are distractible and impulsive. Sometimes they are overactive or "hyper." Their difficulty with self-management may or may not include problems with aggression.

Under-controlled Behavior

Aggressive Type	ADD/ADHD
• defiance or oppositionality	• inability to sit still/over-activeness
• aggressiveness/fighting	• failure to complete tasks
• refusal to follow directions	• difficulty following directions
• disrupting class, temper tantrums	• inattentiveness
• impulsive behavior	• impulsive behavior
• destructiveness	• stealing
• stealing	

TABLE 4.2

Children who show these types of behaviors are likely to be difficult and disrupt the family and the classroom. While some children fit behaviors listed in both categories, many fit only one or the other. It is important to distinguish those who have difficulty with attention and distractibility but are able to control and manage aggression and anger, and vice versa. The strategies for these different behavioral patterns are distinct, and thus assessment of the actual behaviors needs to be carefully delineated.

CASE STUDY: Enrico -- aggressive, oppositional

■ Enrico has a history of becoming aggressive and defiant when given directions and sometimes openly refuses to do as he is asked, directing considerable hostility toward his foster mother. If his brother teases him, Enrico becomes very angry and often responds with aggression, including hitting or kicking. These incidents usually occur while playing outdoors, but they also have been reported at school. Although this behavior does not occur every day, it happens with enough frequency (a few times per week) and is sufficiently disruptive that his mother cannot ignore it. Enrico has few friends and hangs out at school with other students who have a tendency to get into trouble with teachers and administrators for similar behavior.

Case discussion

Enrico is demonstrating under-controlled or externalized aggressive behavior that is a problem at home and in the classroom and also consigns him to a peer group that serves to reinforce his behavior. For many oppositional children, defiance to authority is an effort to maintain a sense of personal control in situations that make them feel vulnerable. Often this reflects negative experiences with parents who have not provided their child with enough sense of control or have responded punitively to the child's seeking autonomy. These children also have difficulty sharing with other children, as they feel the need to control the situation to avoid the feeling of vulnerability that comes with shared control. Such children, because of underlying insecurity, also are very sensitive to name calling and other small slights.

CASE STUDY: Andrea -- distractible, impulsive

Andrea tends to be very distractible in class, so that when multiple activities are occurring at one time, or someone walks into the room, she loses track of what she is doing. This often results in her not finishing her work. In addition, she is quite impulsive, resulting in several of her answers on written materials being incorrect, even though she knows the right answer when given one-on-one help. When given assignments, she often completes only about half before she gets lost or disorganized. She has few friends because they tire of her apparent immaturity and constant disruptive behavior.

Case discussion

Andrea is showing under-controlled behaviors typical of ADD/ ADHD patterns. She is disruptive in the classroom because she has difficulties managing her behavior sufficiently to function academically and socially. Children who are prenatally drug-exposed often show similar patterns of behavior. ADD/ADHD experts believe these problems are a result of a biochemical disorder of the brain that is largely hereditary. Our research indicates that prenatal drug exposure may affect neurotransmitter functioning in a manner that is similar to the changes found with ADD/ADHD. Thus, while the cause of the behavioral problems associated with ADD/ADHD and prenatal drug exposure probably are different, the results appear to be quite similar.

Mixed behaviors

Often children do not show only one type of behavior but show signs of both types of behaviors. We refer to these patterns as "mixed," i.e., those that are not clearly of only the under-controlled or over-controlled type. However, under-controlled behavior patterns may overshadow over-controlled patterns because they are, by definition, disruptive in nature. Therefore, it should not be assumed that internalizing problems are not present just because a child displays only under-controlled patterns. For the parent or teacher, it is important to try to determine what behavioral pattern is most characteristic of the child and then begin to develop an intervention.

CASE STUDY: Bobby -- withdrawal, social isolation

Bobby is a quiet and shy seven-year-old boy who has very few friends. He did not have nice clothes and was unkempt when he arrived at his foster family's home. Bobby's foster brothers and many of his peers tease him and call him names. At home, Bobby spends most of his time alone. At school, when the class is divided into groups to work on a project, members of Bobby's group have been heard making unkind remarks loud enough for everyone to hear. At times, both at home and at school, Bobby is provoked and becomes aggressive toward others. Usually, the behavior is brief, but it does add to his difficulties.

Case discussion

In this situation, Bobby shows both under-controlled and over-controlled problems, although withdrawal and social isolation predominate. Establishing a "we" feeling and positive group identity, whether at home or at school, is the best solution for peer rejection problems. In families and classrooms where prosocial values such as self-control, self-discipline, and the need to care for one's self and for one another are taught, the frequency of peer rejection problems is minimized. Teaching simple, clear values is especially important for children from drug-abusing families, since they often are victims of social and emotional isolation. Such families seldom offer adaptive alternatives to inappropriate behavior, so the child does not know how to respond in social situations.

Children who were prenatally exposed to drugs often exhibit a mixed behavioral picture. They can have difficulty managing their anger in addition to problems with distractibility and impulsive behavior. However, these children also frequently experience high levels of anxiety and feel depressed. In addition, thought problems and some types of social problems do not fit easily into this categorization of over-controlled and under-controlled. Thus, as we view a child and her behavioral difficulties, we must individualize our conceptual approach to understanding the child's behavior.

■   Nilda never seems to finish an assignment. She cannot stay in her seat. She is constantly getting up to go out to the hall or to the window to see what is going on. She almost never gets back on task after a distraction.

Case discussion

This is an example of *under-controlled/attention* behavior. Nilda is easily distracted, is unable to sit still and fails to complete tasks. While these behaviors are characteristic of children with ADD, they also are frequently seen in substance-exposed children. Although teaching a child who is distractible to self-monitor her level of attention may work with an older child, interventions for primary-age children should be more environmental, since younger children generally are not developmentally ready to benefit from direct cognitive interventions. Providing the child with a study area at home or a study carrel at school, frequently monitoring the child's work, and giving the child headphones to play white noise or soft music to block out distractions are beneficial strategies for children who are easily drawn off task.

■   Lucy has outbursts of anger when her requests are not immediately met. When reprimanded she becomes sullen or pouts or tries to lay blame on someone else. She asks for help, but when the teacher tries to explain the assignment she hums, stares out the window and taps her pencil on the desk. In group situations she is very controlling. If she cannot be the "leader" all the time she refuses to participate and withdraws from the group. She is always the last to get in line and often pretends not to hear instructions even when they are directed specifically at her.

Case discussion

Lucy's behavior is referred to as "mixed" because her behavior is not clearly under-controlled or over-controlled. Children rarely show only one type of behavior and may show many signs of both types. The child of an addicted parent comes from a home environment that is inconsistent or in constant conflict and has lived in a world that is often unreliable and unpredictable. Children in this type of home feel confused as to how to please their parents and how to respond to social situations appropriately. Often such children try to establish a sense of control over their lives by resisting external controls. Generally, techniques that encourage children to express their feelings directly will help them develop more positive communication skills. By allowing a child more appropriate choices and options, parents and teachers can develop the child's confidence that she has a role in deciding what she does. Thus she can start to have a sense of control over her life.

CASE STUDY: Martin -- aggressive

Martin is eating dinner with the family. His brother accidentally brushes by Martin as he sits at the table, causing Martin's napkin to fall on the floor. Martin jumps out of his seat and pushes his brother to the floor. Martin also displays this behavior frequently at school on the playground and during group work.

Case discussion

Martin's reaction represents characteristics of under-controlled behavior with aggressiveness and impulsivity. Most often, a child's hostile aggressive behavior is a result of modeling by parents. Our studies have shown substance-exposed children to be at high risk for exposure to violence. The children's birth parents often have been hostile and abusive to each other and frequently used excessive physical punishment as a means of discipline. Thus, rather than teaching skills of conflict resolution, how to define and verbalize feelings, social problem solving, and self-management, drug-abusing parents often teach their children by example that "a good offense is the best defense."

In addition, many drug-exposed children are hypersensitive to sensory input. This may cause a child to erroneously perceive non-threatening contact as threatening. Such children often respond to even small contacts as if they were threats to their safety. Add to this the fact that there is a greater likelihood for overall impulsive behavior and a low threshold for frustration in the drug-exposed child, and you will see the type of response Martin displays.

CASE STUDY: Brian -- withdrawn

Brian is a very quiet first-grader who spends most of his time alone. He does not join in any group activities and stands on the edge of the playground watching other children play. In the classroom he quietly sits at his desk, often sucking his thumb and gazing into space. He has never brought in items for show-and-tell and does not volunteer any answers or participate in class discussions.

Case discussion

Brian is an example of an internalized-withdrawn child who is likely quite shy. He appears to be unhappy and detached. He is withdrawn from others and has very few friends. Children like Brian often are not identified because they are compliant and cooperative in the classroom and at home. Substance-exposed children often withdraw or lapse into daydreaming as an attempt to escape from their anxieties. They often have a poor self-image and negative expectations of themselves and others as a result of failure or mistreatment.

CASE STUDY: Yolanda -- defeatist

Yolanda is of average ability but appears to make very little effort to do her homework. She complains that assignments are too hard before even attempting them. When her foster mother gives her individual attention, she finds Yolanda is very capable of doing the work assigned. But Yolanda gets frustrated and disgusted very easily; instead of trying to solve a problem she gives up, convincing herself she cannot handle it and saying she is "stupid."

Case discussion

Yolanda tends to internalize her feelings of anger and helplessness and thus sets up a pattern of failure that serves to reconfirm her beliefs. She has a low self-image and is defeated before she starts. When she begins a task she applies very little effort and gives up as soon as she encounters any difficulty. Yolanda's behavior is typical of the low frustration tolerance and organizational difficulties exhibited in children who have been substance-exposed.

CHAPTER

5

A Theoretical Basis for Behavioral Change

The sea at dusk glows with a strange light, frost forms on the windowpane in an unusual pattern, and the soup fails to thicken on the stove, and specialists tell us why.

B. F. Skinner: Beyond Freedom and Dignity, 1971, p 32.

When children exhibit behavioral or emotional difficulties, it is common for parents to expect that knowing the cause will help them to develop methods to deal with the problems. It also is common for adults to assume the problems are the product of some inherent characteristics of the child or of a dysfunctional family background. However, viewing the child as the sole or primary source of behavioral problems is inappropriate. Instead, we should consider multiple sources of influence and how these influences come together to produce the behavior we see.

In this chapter, we will present a theory that can help us understand children's behaviors, especially behaviors that have a biologic component, as is the case in alcohol- and drug-exposed children. We will then use this theoretical basis to develop strategies that can help a child learn to manage his behavior. We cannot present specific interventions that will work with every child. Nor can we give you a set of clear-cut rules to follow. But we can help you think through the situations you face as you deal with your child's difficult behaviors. No expert can give you the answer; you need to select those strategies that work for you and your child.

$SORC_i ... C_d$

When developing strategies to change behavior, it is helpful to think of the continuum of factors that precede and follow the observable behavior and the powerful patterns shaped through childhood that produce that behavior. To this end, we will build a conceptual model around $SORC_i...C_d$: Stimulus, Organism, Response, immediate Consequence, distant Consequence.

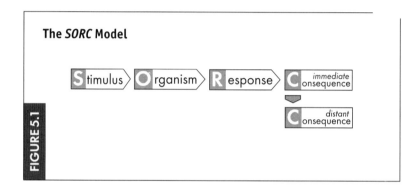

The *SORC* Model

FIGURE 5.1

The stimulus can be any of a number of biological drives (hunger, thirst) or environmental factors (smell, sight) that set off a chain of responses that result in the manifest behavior. Hunger usually will result in eating. A sudden loud noise will pull a child off task and cause him to leave his schoolwork. The organism is the child's cognitive process that acknowledges, recognizes, and interprets the stimulus. Hearing his mother pull into the driveway will bring a young child running to the window to look for her. The consideration and interpretation of the stimulus selects the individual's response from his repertoire of behaviors. The immediate consequence of the response is the satisfaction of a physical or psychological need. The distant consequence is the long-term impact of the behavior.

The newborn infant responds mainly through reflex. There is very little interpretation of stimuli. With maturation, experience, and cognitive input, the child develops as an organism. He builds on past experiences to recognize and interpret stimuli and to select his behavioral response. He becomes aware of two types of immediate consequences: physical, such as the recognition that eating relieves feelings of hunger, and social, such as a parent's approval for appropriate behavior. The immediate consequences, both physical and social, reinforce the behavior. In contrast, distant consequences have no impact on reinforcing or maintaining the child's behavior. In this way, children are not much different from many adults. Having a loaf of warm bread and a platter of fresh butter set on the table before you most likely will result in your buttering the bread and eating it. This response will occur as you seek the immediate consequence of enjoying the taste of the bread and butter. Unfortunately, the distant consequence, a high cholesterol level and risk of heart disease, will come in time but has little impact on preventing you from eating the bread and butter.

In attempts to change behavior, it must be recognized that the immediate consequence will almost always overshadow the distant consequence. Thus, knowing that eating too much butter will result in heart trouble in the future does not keep you from eating the butter now. Your focus is on the immediate consequence – the taste of the butter. A group of Olympic-bound athletes were once asked the question, "If you were given the choice of winning a gold medal but dying in five years, or winning no medal but living a full life span, which would you choose?" Almost every athlete chose the immediate consequence, the gold medal.

With this in mind, it is easy to understand why our model for intervention becomes *SORC*, dropping the final C – for distant consequence – since distant consequences do not provide an opportunity for intervention. For instance, children with a low tolerance for frustration and anxiety become easily over-stimulated and develop high levels of energy and tension that must be immediately discharged. The high-energy child who responds to a disruption by jumping out of his chair is doing so in order to achieve the immediate consequence of releasing this tension. Threatening a distant consequence of punishment, even if it is to occur right after the behavior, does not have an effect on his behavior and in fact can increase the frustration and anxiety. The child seeks only the immediate consequence, the release of tension.

As we try to understand and address the behavioral regulation problems of drug-exposed children, we will use the SORC model – stimulus, organism, response, immediate consequence – to develop intervention strategies. From this model, we will see why attempting to externally control a child's behavior, especially through distant consequences, will not succeed and why teaching the child to internally manage his behavior will have longer lasting benefit.

Stimulus: Biologic drives and environmental factors

At birth, the newborn's biologic drives – hunger, thirst – provide the stimulus for a reflexive behavioral response that results in a physical consequence - usually pleasure or relief of discomfort. Immediately at birth, however, the environment begins to impinge on the purely reactive world of the newborn, and the child begins to integrate sensory information from the environment. Through the process of maturation, environmental factors play an ever-increasing role in stimulating the child's behavior. However, although the normal newborn almost immediately begins to integrate stimuli from the environment to trigger behavioral responses, drug- and alcohol-exposed infants continue to react reflexively, unable to process sensory information or to take in and utilize the stimuli, especially if there is more than one stimulus at a time.

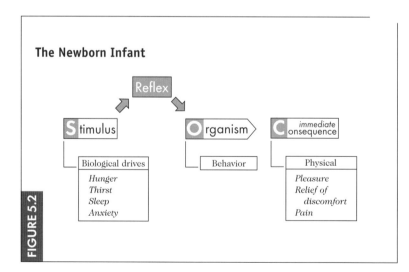

FIGURE 5.2

The Newborn Infant

Reflex

Stimulus → **O**rganism → **C** immediate onsequence

Biological drives	Behavior	Physical
Hunger		*Pleasure*
Thirst		*Relief of*
Sleep		*discomfort*
Anxiety		*Pain*

Environmental factors for the newborn emanate almost exclusively from the primary caretaker and the immediate home environment. As the child grows older, his world expands, and environmental factors become the characteristics of the child's home, family relationships, neighborhood and school climate. It is important to remember that each child is embedded within many layers of environment, and that the influences may be indirect. For example, not only are children affected by the behavior of their parents, but their parents, in turn, are affected by the neighborhood environment, economic stress, and other environmental conditions. The larger school environment in which a classroom is embedded similarly affects the child directly, but also affects the child through the impact the larger environment has on the teacher and other school personnel who work with the child. Children always bring the influence of the larger environment to bear on their behavior, learning and relationships.

Home and family relationships

Ineffective parenting, including difficulty setting limits or use of inappropriate punishment, can affect a child's behavior as well as her response to authority. If parents are using drugs, the home environment likely is unpredictable and lacks structure. In addition, drug-using parents are usually struggling to manage the larger ecological conditions associated with poverty, including many children in the home, unsafe neighborhoods, violence, lack of community resources, including poor medical care and few recreational opportunities, and concerns about meeting the family's basic needs. All these conditions can contribute to disorganization in the child's life and escalate problems in behavioral regulation that may show up long after the child has been moved to foster or adoptive care.

Classroom factors

Although it is common for adults to attribute the sources of behavioral problems to the child and home, there is ample research evidence to indicate the classroom environment contributes significantly to behavioral problems. Consideration of the classroom environment thus is critical for the successful management of behavioral problems. It also is much easier to change current circumstances that contribute to a problem than it is to change a child's characteristics. For example, if a child has an attention problem that is intensified in a situation where he is easily distracted, it will be much more effective to change the distracting situation than attempt to train the child to be more attentive. Although the child still may have the attention problem, it will be manifested to a much lesser extent if the situation can be changed.

Similarly, by addressing some classroom factors, the school often can improve behavior and learning for all children in a classroom by taking steps to alleviate common situational difficulties:

- Large class size or grouping problems
- Structure or arrangement of the classroom
- Unclear or inappropriate expectations for behavior
- Tasks or instructional conditions that are inappropriate for the children
- Presence of several children who present management difficulties

It is instructive to examine one of these situational factors that may contribute to a child's behavior - unrealistic expectations from adults. If a child is expected to do more than he can do, he may become frustrated, and no amount of coaxing, coercion, or application of management techniques will enable him to do something he cannot do. A child may react negatively to the pressure by showing behavior such as refusal to cooperate, disruptive behavior, inattentiveness, or inconsistent performance. If adults are not aware that a child is being asked to do something beyond his current skill level, such behavior is assumed to be willful disobedience. Often tailoring expectations to realistically fit a child's abilities may solve the problem.

CASE STUDY: Alexander

■ Alexander is a child who is very susceptible to changes in his environment and responds to these changes with very impulsive behavior. In fact, toward the end of the school year, Alexander's third grade teacher called his adoptive mother. "You have to get

Alexander on Ritalin, or I will not keep him in my classroom." This was one of several calls that year, and Alexander's mother sought help from the Child Study Center. Alexander had been born to a mother who used cocaine and alcohol throughout pregnancy. She gave her son up for adoption immediately after birth, and Alexander had fared well in his adoptive home. However, by two years of age, it was clear that Alexander was easily distracted, especially by visual stimuli. His adoptive mother, a special education teacher, was able to manage his distractibility and by the time he entered kindergarten, Alexander was performing well academically. Things started to fall apart by third grade, however, as learning moved from the concrete to the more abstract.

On the day of the incident in question, the teacher had been in the middle of a class about dolphins, when Alexander suddenly yelled out, "We have *Charlotte's Web* at home!" This outburst pulled the entire classroom of children off task and resulted in a level of chaos that the teacher could not bring back under control. The teacher was furious with Alexander, and blamed him for once again taking away valuable class time. She resolved that unless Alexander was placed on Ritalin, she would not allow him back in class.

Case discussion

In reviewing the day with the teacher, we learned that prior to the start of class that morning, she had opened her mail and found a poster announcing a new edition of *Charlotte's Web*. She tacked the poster up on the wall, called the class to order, and proceeded. However, that poster was a distraction for all of the children in the classroom, most of whom were wondering what it was doing up there. Alexander was particularly distracted, and as he worked harder and harder to stay on task and listen to the teacher, his internal tension continued to build until he could control himself no longer.

Alexander's outburst relieved the pent-up energy, but did not win him the affection of his teacher. On the other hand, if the teacher had explained to the children, prior to starting the class, that the poster was there to announce that they would soon be reading the book *Charlotte's Web*, all of the children would have understood the poster's purpose and the poster would have been given meaning and context for Alexander, minimizing its distracting influence.

■ ■

Organism: Child-specific factors

The organism in the *SORC* model is the child's cognitive acknowledgement, recognition, consideration, and interpretation of a biologic drive or environmental stimulus. This interpretation and consideration of the stimulus selects the child's response from his repertoire of behaviors. The very young infant responds through reflex; there is very little involved in interpretation of the stimulus. In a newborn, lightly stroking the side of the mouth results in a rooting reflex, allowing the infant to find the nipple and to initiate sucking. With maturation, the rooting reflex disappears and is re-placed by a learned response: the smell of the mother's milk will cause the infant to seek the nipple and to initiate sucking. The infant has successfully paired the stimulus, the smell of the milk, with the appropriate response. He no longer is merely reactive, but has successfully made a connection between two discrete events, and his behavior has become goal-oriented.

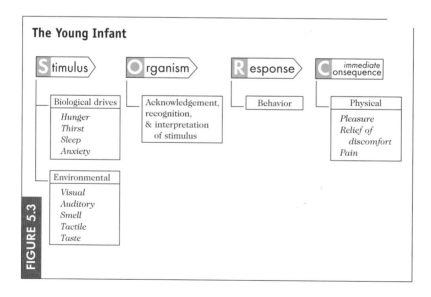

The Young Infant

FIGURE 5.3

Ch5: A Theoretical Basis for Behavioral Change

If a child is not able to recognize and learn logical pairings, then he will continue to operate in a reactive rather than a goal-oriented mode. In fact, as described in previous chapters, the nerve pathways of children who have been exposed to alcohol or drugs prenatally do not develop appropriately during fetal life. If the nerve pathways do not develop, there is a failure in the communication system between the different parts of the brain, hindering appropriate interpretation of stimuli. This is only one example of a variety of child-specific factors that can increase a child's vulnerability to developing behavioral problems that often are made worse by home and family difficulties.

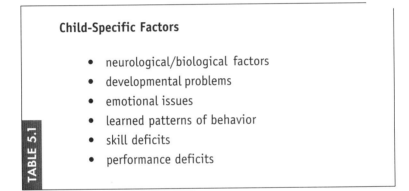

Child-Specific Factors

- neurological/biological factors
- developmental problems
- emotional issues
- learned patterns of behavior
- skill deficits
- performance deficits

TABLE 5.1

Neurological/biological factors

The behavioral difficulties of children who were exposed to alcohol or drugs prenatally can best be understood at the level of the organism. Prenatal alcohol exposure interferes with the processing of information. Prenatal drug exposure affects dopamine receptor levels at nerve endings in the brain, preventing appropriate recognition and interpretation of environmental stimuli, especially if the child is being distracted by other factors in the environment. The child reaches his threshold for stimulation quickly, becomes easily over-stimulated, and reacts impulsively in an attempt to release escalating tension. By striking out, the child's tension is relieved, but he creates havoc in the home or classroom.

There may be a tendency by some to assume that if behavioral problems have a neurological or biological basis, little can be done other than to try to control the children using medication or through external behavioral control. However, there is ample research evidence and experience to indicate that through therapeutic intervention, behavioral problems can be greatly reduced or managed through other strategies. Children with attention deficit problems have been taught methods that significantly improve their attention. Additionally, many of the problems experienced by substance-exposed children can be improved by a simple change in the parent's attitude. This change may be brought about through increased understanding of the difficulties that substance-exposed children have in managing frustration and stimulation and in regulating and organizing themselves.

Developmental and health problems

Developmental problems or delays, which may or may not have an identifiable neurological or biological basis, may also be a source of behavioral problems. Developmental disorders such as delayed speech and language capabilities often lead to social withdrawal, heightened frustration resulting in tantrums or outbursts, and academic difficulties. Other developmental disorders, such as autism, are diagnosed because of the existence of disruptive or unusual behaviors and social interaction. As with neurologically or biologically based behavioral problems, behaviors that reflect developmental delays or disorders can be influenced by how the parent handles them. Further, many of these behaviors can be effectively addressed with management techniques that reflect an understanding of the underlying problem.

Clearly, it is important to make certain that children who come from a drug-affected environment are properly screened for health problems. Vision and hearing deficiencies impede social and emotional development, speech and language development, and behavior. Poor growth attributed to prenatal alcohol or drug exposure may in fact be due to urinary tract infection or low thyroid levels. In any case, an early health screening can be critical in ensuring that each child has the opportunity to reach her full potential.

Emotional issues

A child's emotional problems, such as anxiety, depression, anger, and hostility, can be a source of behavior difficulties. Many times, the root of these problems is not clear, although they often reflect other domains of problems, such as environmental issues. Drug-exposed children are even more vulnerable to the toll of emotional stress because they have difficulty with the increased tension such stress creates. They quickly become disorganized but do not understand their loss of control and are confused and frightened by it. Such children are frequently identified as "willfully disobedient" or "behavior problems" by the foster or adoptive parent who, by misunderstanding the nature of the child's problem, causes increased anxiety and stress in the child. Emotional problems often factor into disruptive behaviors, although other children with emotional problems can be easily overlooked because they are withdrawn or quiet.

Learned patterns of behavior

All behavior is purposeful. When children demonstrate behavioral problems, they often are looking for a particular outcome. If successful, the inappropriate behavior is incorporated into the child's repertoire of behaviors. The parent who can identify the function of a child's behavior will be able to adjust the environment or the relational interactions with the child and improve the child's behavior.

While behavioral problems may reflect learned functions, it is important to remember that for some children behavior may reflect the child's effort to cope with neurological/biological or developmental vulnerabilities. Above all, it must be recognized that there always is a reason for every behavior. When a child is behaving negatively, it is more productive for the parent to try to determine what the child hopes to achieve with the misbehavior rather than engage in punitive measures. If a reason can be found, then it is possible to develop interventions that can successfully address this underlying source of the behavior.

The Function of Behavior

Behavior	Others' perceptions of behavior	Function
Seeks control of events and situations	Non-cooperative, obstinate	Power / control
Seeks to avoid a task or escape a consequence or negative situation, seeks to avoid threatening situations or feelings of vulnerability	Shy, withdrawn	Protection / escape / avoidance
Tries to set self apart from others, seeks to be the focus	Selfish, self-centered	Attention
Over-friendly, does not recognize boundaries	Intrusive	Interpersonal connection
Seeks reward or enjoyment at own direction	Uncaring of others' feelings, lacks empathy	Gratification
Seeks settlement of differences or to "get even"	Aggressive, mean	Justice

TABLE 5.2

Skill deficits: Can the child do it?

Skill deficits refer to the child's lacking the skills needed to perform the desired tasks. Reasons for skill deficits include misguided teaching and modeling at home, developmental delays, or lack of opportunity to learn the desired skills. Some substance-exposed children may enter a foster or adoptive family without ever having such simple experiences as hearing stories or rhymes, learning colors and numbers, or naming the objects in their environment.

Some vulnerable or high-risk children, including those prenatally exposed to drugs, may have more difficulty learning certain types of skills that are needed for prosocial behavior due to their impulsive behavior, low frustration tolerance, and a tendency toward disorganized behavior.

For skill deficits, the challenge is to determine what the specific deficits are and find ways to teach and develop them. It also should be remembered that what is assumed to be a performance deficit, may, in fact, be a skill deficit. The child may not be misbehaving intentionally; he simply does not know how to do what is appropriate. The behavior he exhibits is what he knows how to do, even though it can have negative consequences.

For some children skill deficits may be rather small and need little remediation, while others may need much more effort. For example, the prenatally exposed boy at school who has difficulty lining up to go to lunch or cannot get his books together to go home at the end of the day may need to be physically walked through the process several times until it becomes an automatic part of his behavioral repertoire. The girl who cannot keep herself organized to complete work when she does not have someone working with her or gets side-tracked when asked to prepare for bed needs extra help organizing her tasks initially, and then regular check-ins from the teacher and parent to ensure that she has kept herself on target. Identification and remediation of skill deficits often will correct and eliminate many problem behaviors because the child will now know what to do and what is expected, especially when given well-placed reminders and positive reinforcement and praise.

Performance deficits: Will the child do it?

Performance deficits refer to those skills that a child has and knows how to perform, but, for any of a variety of reasons, does not perform them. Many children have the skills, but other interfering factors prevent the desired behaviors from being demonstrated. For instance, the child who cannot read social cues will not respond appropriately when approached by another child. In order for the parent to address performance deficits, he must understand why the child is not performing as desired, respond sympathetically to this problem, and help the child understand that negative behaviors are inappropriate and that more benefit will come from appropriate, or "prosocial," behaviors.

Performance deficits may be characterized by highly variable behavior, such as when a child does well in one situation but not in another. It may be that the child has a performance deficit in the classroom, but is fine at home because his mother provides one-on-one structure, consistency, and personal interest as he works. However, variability in performance may also be hiding a skill deficit due to the fact that the level of skill required for success in one setting is not adequate for another setting. Again, the child may be able to do his math problems at home with his mother by his side, but when left to complete the same material on his own, he is unable to do so because of organizational deficits. Therefore, the distinction between performance and skill deficits can sometimes be quite difficult to assess. However, it is important to make this distinction because your approach will be different for skill deficits as compared with performance deficits.

In general, the most successful approach to addressing a performance deficit is to identify an alternative, desired behavior and try to strengthen it through teaching, positive reinforcement, and helping the child feel good about her appropriate behavior.

Response: Children's misbehavior as messages

Although it is common for adults to react to children's misbehavior by seeking to control, change, or eliminate it, it is more useful to consider misbehavior as a message that something is wrong and the child does not know how to correct it. Usually the behavior is functional in some way — that is, it helps a child cope with anxiety, anger, frustration, over-stimulation or other negative feelings. Because the behavior is functional, parents will be unsuccessful in their efforts to eliminate it unless they help the child find alternative behaviors that are more appropriate or adaptive.

There are many other messages children can send through their behavior, and it may be difficult to determine what they are trying to communicate. Usually, however, through experience with that child, the parent can read the message, figure out the function of the behavior and take some action. The important thing to remember is that a message is there, and if you can figure it out, you may well be on your way to solving the problem quickly.

Behavioral Messages

Behavior	Message
Withdrawal	"I'm scared." "No one likes me." "I'm sad." "I don't know how to reach out to others."
Shyness	"I'm overwhelmed." "I'm unsure of myself." "I can't cope with this."
Submissiveness	"I don't feel good about myself." "I don't know what to do."
Aggression	"I can't do this, it's too hard." "I'm not being treated fairly." "I'm frustrated." "I'm angry." "I can't cope with this."
Inattention	"I'm bored." "I don't know what to do." "I need a break." "I got distracted."
Refusal to comply	"I'm mad and I don't want to be here." "This is not fair." "If I try, I'll fail."
Non-completion of tasks	"I don't know how to do this." "This is too hard." "I don't know how to organize this." "I got distracted and forgot what I was doing."

TABLE 5.3

Consequences: Immediate vs. distant

The child can recognize only the feelings and relief that occur within the immediate context of a behavioral response. Attempting to use distant consequences, especially in the guise of threats, will not work. Just as cigarette smokers continue to smoke for the immediate consequence of taste and relaxation and ignore the distant consequence of lung cancer, children with regulatory difficulties will seek ways to relieve the anxiety, tension, and arousal they are feeling, ignoring the distant consequence of failing in their school work.

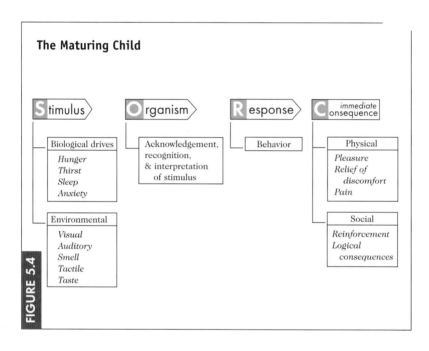

The Maturing Child

FIGURE 5.4

The key to behavioral intervention, then, is to address immediate consequences, remembering that the child will quickly come to recognize two forms of immediate consequences: physical and social. Physical consequences signal pleasure and relief of the biologic drives. However, the social consequences soon become the stronger of these two categories, for children crave approval from their parents. If the immediate consequences provided by the parents are consistent and logical, the child will begin to incorporate the parent into himself. In this way, parents are able to pass their own values on to their children. Adolescents test the bounds of parental approval, seeking boundaries for behavior and constantly needing to reaffirm those boundaries. They work through their emerging sense of identity by first understanding what their identity is not. With maturity, they begin to ask, "Is that behavior consistent with who I am?"

Two traditional tools that parents use for communicating immediate consequences and that have been widely used and researched by behavioral psychologists for learning and behavior change are reinforcement and punishment. Most parents are at least somewhat familiar with these ideas and use variations of them daily. In working with a child with behavioral regulation difficulties, we will expand on these two concepts to guide management interventions.

What is reinforcement?

Reinforcement and punishment can be thought of as two ends of the same stick. On one end is reinforcement, which seeks to affect behavior and learning by increasing a desired behavior or behavioral response so it is more likely to occur. Like reinforcing wood or concrete to make it more durable and more resistant to change, so behavioral reinforcement strengthens the targeted behavior. Reinforcement takes place when an object the child likes (such as a novelty sticker or verbal praise) increases the frequency of an appropriate behavior (such as completing an assigned task). When the appropriate behavior occurs, the reinforcer (sticker, praise), must follow it. If the behavior (completing the task) increases in frequency or duration after the reinforcer is given, then reinforcement has occurred. Reinforcers include everything from material items to privileges, attention, praise, power, and choices.

What is punishment?

In contrast to reinforcement, and on the other end of the stick, is punishment, which seeks to decrease the occurrence of an inappropriate or undesirable behavior. In a case in which a child is making noises at the dinner table, the parent may reprimand her in an attempt to stop or decrease the behavior. If the child stops making noises after the reprimand (or makes the noise less frequently) then the reprimand is an effective punishment. Time outs, verbal reprimands, and extra chores around the house are all examples of punishment.

Punishment often does not provide an effective intervention with the drug-exposed child. This is likely due to the high anxiety levels and skill deficits often present in drug-exposed children and the fact that punishment increases tension and anxiety, which can then cause an escalation in the undesired behavior. For example, John is making tapping noises with his pencil in class and ignores the teacher's requests that he stop. He is sent to timeout, where his behavior actually gets worse because as he struggles to manage the increased tension, he becomes increasingly agitated and disruptive.

Positive and negative reinforcement and punishment

There are two broad classes of interventions utilizing the reinforcement/ punishment model: positive reinforcement/positive punishment and negative reinforcement/negative punishment. In this model, positive means the act of providing something in response to a behavior, either a reinforcer (sticker) or punishment (extra homework), while negative means removing something.

Positive reinforcement: Positive reinforcement occurs when an event or object that the child likes (the reinforcer) is given following an appropriate behavior, which should cause an increase in frequency.

Jamal and his mother are at odds. Jamal complains that his mother is always picking on him, and his mother complains that Jamal is constantly running around, disturbing his brother and sister, and rarely doing his homework without continual prompting. Jamal is interested in his baseball card collection. Jamal's mother works out a system in which Jamal earns points for every homework assignment he turns in on time. His mother tracks the points and exchanges them for money that Jamal can use to purchase baseball cards. Jamal completes his homework on time.

Positive reinforcement has occurred because the frequency of the appropriate behavior has increased in response to the presence of the reinforcer, the points for baseball cards.

Negative reinforcement: Negative reinforcement occurs when an event or object the child dislikes is removed after the child shows the appropriate behavior.

> *Tom fails to independently complete class assignments that he is capable of doing. The teacher stands near his desk, prompting him to complete the work. Tom does not like the teacher's frequent prompts, and he begins completing his work. In turn, the teacher leaves him alone, and he continues to work to avoid future prompting.*

Negative reinforcement has occurred because the frequency of the appropriate behavior increased in response to the removal of the unwanted prompt, the teacher standing at his desk.

Positive punishment: Positive punishment occurs when a disliked event or object is introduced to the child to reduce an inappropriate behavior.

> *Eric is playing around and not listening to the coach during practice. The coach tells him to do 50 push-ups because of his inappropriate behavior.*

Positive punishment has occurred because the coach seeks to decrease the frequency of the behavior through the presence of the punishment, the push-ups.

Negative punishment: Negative punishment occurs when a desired event or object is removed, resulting in a decrease of unwanted behavior. Removing privileges, the most common use of negative punishment, can be effective for reducing misbehavior, especially in older children.

Tamara continually talks to her friends during class, despite frequent reminders to stop. The teacher punishes her by not allowing her to go outside during recess.

Negative punishment has occurred because the teacher is attempting to decrease an undesirable behavior by removing a desired event or response, recess.

Although it may seem to the parent that there is little difference between these four categories of intervention, there is a world of difference from the child's perception. "Time-outs" are a good example. In some situations, time outs, a form of positive punishment, can be an effective intervention for reducing unwanted behavior by helping children calm down and not receive attention for undesired behavior. For drug-exposed children, however, a time out often elevates the arousal level, making it more difficult for the child to calm down and reorganize his behavior.

───────────────────────────────── **CASE STUDY: John**

┃
■   John was having difficulty with an assignment and was using his pencil to count. He became completely frustrated and was unable to respond to his teacher's repeated verbal requests to stop tapping his pencil. When placed in time out, his frustration and anxiety escalated. He finally lost control and threw a book at the teacher.

John perceived the time out given by his teacher as a form of punishment for misbehavior. His tapping was the only way John knew to reduce his increasing levels of anxiety and tension. If John had had permission to take a "cool down" period whenever he wanted, that is, removing himself from his work and going to a quiet corner of the classroom, he would have been able to calm his rising tensions and return to his work. Also, allowing John to make the decision as to when he needed a "cool down" time would empower him to manage his own behavior rather than relying on the external controls handed down by his teacher. Drug-exposed children, with their heightened levels of anxiety and depression, will respond far more favorably to proactive interventions, such as self-determined "cool down" periods, as opposed to reactive punishment, such as a forced time out.

■ ▌

Interactions between stimulus, organism, response and consequence

Interactions between the stimulus (environmental factors) and the organism (child-specific factors) can create particular problems for the foster or adoptive parent. If a child has a tendency to be hyperactive and inattentive (child-specific factors) and came from a home in which the parents used drugs and did not provide adequate structure and limit-setting for their child (environmental factors), the child may show some of the distractibility and impulsive behavior that are characteristic of a child with attention deficit problems. In this situation, however, it is likely the environment of the birth home exacerbated these behavioral tendencies and made the problems worse.

It also is important to recognize that a stimulus has influence only if it is noticed; not all stimuli are noticed by a child. In fact, the drug-exposed child who becomes easily overloaded will "shut down" to protect himself (organism) from over stimulation. Thus he selectively blocks out stimuli that a parent may be presenting. The child may seem to be stubborn or obstinate (response), but in reality he is protecting himself (immediate consequence) from being overwhelmed by his environment. Unfortunately, if the home is particularly chaotic or the parent does not understand the child's observable behavior, the parent will scold the child (immediate consequence), over stimulating him further and causing him to withdraw even more (response).

The Mature Child

As the child matures, consequences become developmentally more sophisticated. The *physical* consequences that signal relief of biologic drives give way to *social* consequences, that is, the parents' approval and reinforcement of appropriate behaviors. The feelings of personal gratification that come with approval and reinforcement drive the child toward goal-oriented behavior, as the child seeks further approval and reinforcement. Thus, thought (*O* in our model) becomes a stimulus for appropriate behavior. If a child's self-motivated behavior is consistently awarded with approval and reinforcement, the child gains self-esteem ("I'm O.K.!") and self-efficacy ("I can do it!"). Through this process, these *personal consequences* grow in importance, and the child develops values and a sense of self-identity ("I am myself.") that will continue to drive goal-directed behavior. This is a key point as we begin to develop intervention strategies that focus on internal management rather than external control of behavior for children affected by prenatal exposure to drugs and alcohol.

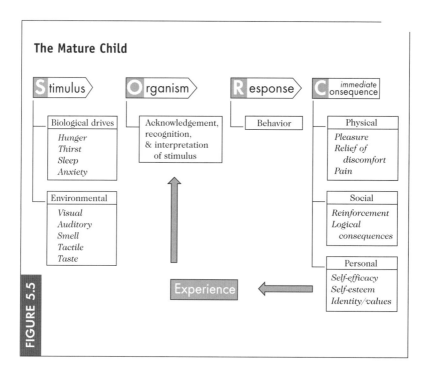

FIGURE 5.5

Developing an Intervention Strategy: Internal Management vs. External Control

Behavior is shaped by the interaction of the stimulus and the organism. Behavior is maintained and strengthened by consequences. The normal maturational process of behavior is one in which, with age, the child begins to internalize past experiences and behavioral guidelines that he has learned from his parents, communicated through social consequences: approval and reinforcement. Consistent positive social consequences become imbedded in the organism as personal consequences, which then take a role in shaping future goal-directed behavior. From this perspective, it can be appreciated that with maturation, the *SORC* process becomes circular rather than linear.

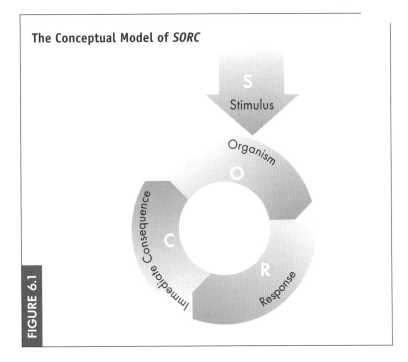

The Conceptual Model of *SORC*

FIGURE 6.1

Children who grow up in a vegetarian home may be asked as adults why they do not eat meat. Their response is simple: "Because it's not the way I was raised." Maturity is when behavioral responses come under control of personal consequences, having been incorporated into the organism as a value. In contrast, for children who have been adopted from a home in which one or both parents used drugs, their addicted parents' need for drugs or alcohol usually took precedence over meeting the needs of their children. Most often the child's parents were focused on "getting high," and the child was perceived as a barrier to that goal. Such parents' interactions with their children tended to be erratic as their drug use impacted their mood, resulting in frequent swings from impatience and anger to disinterest and apathy. Such conditions created a world in which the children's needs were not met, and the environment was unreliable and unpredictable. The children never developed an ordered sense of the universe, and they never made the connections between cause and effect. If children cannot recognize cause and effect relationships, their behavior cannot come under control of social consequences. Thus behavior continues to be reactive, focusing only on physical consequences that relieve discomfort.

Often, foster or adoptive parents may not be aware that a child has been prenatally exposed to alcohol or other drugs, but must respond to behaviors that could (or could not) be the result of exposure. While there are no "unique" interventions for behavioral problems associated with prenatal exposure, children with this history often do not respond to standard child rearing practices. Thus, there is a need for an overarching template for understanding the special problems these children struggle with along with intervention strategies that have proven especially helpful for this population. The goal is to help children learn to manage themselves, rather than to rely on an outside source, such as the adoptive parent, to control their behavior.

Management vs. control

When many parents talk about managing their child, they implicitly or explicitly may equate it with maintaining control of the child. The goal of behavioral control is to suppress or contain undesirable behavior so family or classroom interactions can continue in an orderly manner. However, parents need to empower children to take control of their lives by facilitating their behavioral development, not controlling it. Often, much time is spent developing ways to externally control the behavior of children when what the children need are adults who will empower them through respect, listening, collaboration and problem solving approaches.

From our perspective, management is defined as helping the child to bring behavior under his own control versus continuing to depend on other's interventions. In many cases, parents will focus on trying to control a child's behavior by intervening with immediate or sometimes even distant consequences disguised as threats. As we progress through the *SORC* continuum, we will find that parents have far more intervention points available to them all along the continuum. Especially as children who have been prenatally exposed to drugs enter a new foster or adoptive home, it can be assumed that the structured environment (*stimuli*), the models of prosocial behavior (*organism*), a wide range of behaviors (*response*) and consistent *consequences* were lacking in their biological home. These are the dimensions that help all children succeed, but are especially critical for prenatally exposed children.

CASE STUDY: Johnny

■ Johnny's story illustrates how interventions at all levels of the *SORC* continuum can be effective in managing a child's behavior. "It seems like every day he gets into trouble," Ms. Jones tells the psychologist. "He starts running and then can't stop. Within a few minutes he's running wildly and screaming. Sometimes he pushes his brothers when they are in his way. I have no choice but to send him to his room and punish him. When I do that, though, he sulks for the rest of the day and won't participate in any of the family activities. I tried taking away television privileges, but no matter how many times I do, he does the same thing again the next time he has the chance. None of his brothers wants to play with him anymore because he has to control the play activity, which leads to conflicts and then gets them into trouble."

1. Are Ms. Jones' efforts effective in trying to manage Johnny's behavior? Why or why not?
2. What are some more effective ways to manage Johnny's behavior?

Ms. Jones' use of external threats and confinement to interrupt Johnny's behavior has been unsuccessful. The description of Johnny's behavior suggests he tends to display under-controlled behavior and has difficulty organizing himself, so Ms. Jones attempts to control him by sending him to his room. Although it may be necessary to remove him from a situation temporarily, he does not seem to be learning anything from the approach because he often repeats the pattern. This is the problem with strategies aimed at controlling behavior rather than managing it so that the child learns self-control and how to act appropriately.

Free time can often be an extremely difficult time for children with the kind of regulatory problems often displayed by drug-exposed children. The combination of excitement and lack of structure can make it very difficult for them to calm down and organize their behavior. If a child has organizational difficulties, consider if this is a skill deficit, a performance deficit, or a motivational problem. Think *prevention*. Discuss expectations for play behavior at length prior to letting Johnny go outside with his brothers. Set a clear plan for what he would like to do outside and whom he would like to play with so there is structure for his activity. Talk through what his behavior should look like and what you will do if you notice his behavior is not in keeping with his stated plan. At such a time, Johnny should be removed from the situation or behavior in which he is engaged and provided an alternative spot in which to calm down until he appears ready to manage and organize his behavior again. Give Johnny large amounts of praise as he becomes increasingly successful in managing himself. In the long run, Johnny may even be able to take himself out of situations when he is beginning to feel out of control, so he can give himself a "break" and put himself back in control of himself.

The concept of behavior management versus control is simple but important. As illustrated in the suggestions for managing Johnny, parents should teach children to manage their own behavior through self-control, responsibility, and social skills, just as they help their children with school subjects such as reading and mathematics. Returning to the case of Johnny, Ms. Jones continues her discussion with the psychologist. Trying to understand factors that may have contributed to Johnny's behavior, the psychologist asks about the previous evening.

CASE STUDY: Johnny

■ "Everything went smoothly yesterday after school until dinner time," Ms. Jones recalls. "My husband and I and the boys were eating and talking. Then Johnny got up and started walking around the room, disturbing everyone. I told him to sit down and eat his dinner and he said he didn't like the food, even though I had asked him what he wanted for dinner. I told him that he would have to leave the room, so I sent him to his room and closed the door. He started making noises through the vent. I sent my husband to talk with him. Later, when Johnny returned to the dinner table, he hit one of his brothers because he said he drank some of his milk. I'm afraid I lost my temper and told him that if he didn't want to eat I didn't care what he did as long as he didn't bother anyone else. Then he started making quacking noises, disrupting everyone's dinner. I have told him that he would have to eat alone from now on. I really don't know what to do with him anymore. I have tried every punishment I know, and he doesn't seem to care!"

1. Why does Ms. Jones believe that Johnny is acting out? What other reasons might there be for his behavior?

Ms. Jones appears to think Johnny is acting out in order to bother her or the rest of the family. However, there are many other possibilities to explain this behavior, including Johnny's having difficulty focusing on the task of eating because of a distraction in the room or problems at school.

2. What was the first indication that Johnny was having difficulty managing himself? What could Ms. Jones have done to more successfully manage Johnny's behavior?

*The first indication that Johnny was having difficulty man-
aging himself came when he left his seat and began to walk
around the room. Ms. Jones at that point could have checked
to see that he understood and remembered that dinnertime
was a time for the family to be together and share a meal.*

In this situation, the mother clearly feels frustrated and is using
techniques to suppress and control behavior. Although Ms. Jones
stated that she had let Johnny select the food, Johnny said he did
not like it. Ms. Jones assumes Johnny is willfully not doing something, when his distractibility and low tolerance for frustration seem
to be at the heart of the problem. There are several strategies that
could have been used that likely would have prevented the escalation of problems:

1. Listening carefully to Johnny's communication and responding in a way that lets him know he has been "heard."
2. Recognizing that not all challenging behavior is intentional
   acting out in pursuit of attention for attention's sake.
3. Recognizing that not all children operate at the same level
   and respond to formal explanations and directions in the
   same way.
4. Remembering that there may be more than one explanation
   for Johnny's behavior.
5. Acknowledging the constant need for the parent to balance
   her responsibilities to the family as a whole and the special
   needs of a specific child.

■ ■

Contrasting control vs. management of behavior

Behavior	Control	Management
Johnny gets into fights with his brothers.	Send Johnny to his room.	Talk through the expected behavior with Johnny before he plays with his brothers. This is a response at the level of the *organism*, because this strategy trains Johnny cognitively to anticipate the event.
Johnny gets up and wanders around the room during dinner.	Keep Johnny in his seat.	Make sure dinnertime is clearly organized and struc-tured (managing the *stimulus*) Set a time limit for how long Johnny is expected to be at the table (ten minutes, for example), then permit a short break before he returns for another ten minutes.

TABLE 6.1

The parents' role in behavior management

Much of what is written and practiced in managing children's behavior involves addressing emotional and behavioral problems that have a long history and may require direct interventions to modify. However, another important aspect of addressing problems is to learn more about preventing their occurrence in the first place. In general, it is much more effective to prevent problems than it is to respond to them after they have emerged.

Promoting desired behaviors

There are two key principles of preventive behavior manage-ment: promoting positive, desired behaviors and minimizing disrup-tive behaviors. The home that is prevention-focused will use proce-dures and techniques that focus on both components. It should be remembered, however, that even in the best-managed homes, where sound prevention practices are evident, problem behaviors nevertheless will occur.

Communicating desired behaviors

How often have you heard someone say, "You know better than that!" to a child? As adults we tend to assume that children have been taught what is acceptable and what is not acceptable behavior, but that often is not the case. Children who come from a drug-using environment do not get much helpful feedback on their behavior and often have not learned that logical consequences depend on their behavior. When we work with children we must not only tell them what we don't want them to do, but be very specific about why that behavior is unacceptable and what would be acceptable in that circumstance. Use clearly stated rules and expectations so the child knows what behaviors will earn him positive results and those that will not. Although telling a child what you want is the most logical way to communicate, you can also communicate in a variety of other ways.

To communicate desired behaviors:
- Post a chart of family rules.
- Model appropriate behaviors.
- Remind the children of rules when an individual child breaks a rule.
- Teach and practice the desired behavior (role playing).
- Give feedback to the child about his behavior.
- Show approval of behavior through smiles, hugs, and other positive nonverbal looks or gestures.

Establishing behavioral expectations

Establishing and enforcing behavioral expectations provides clarity and consistency for what the child can expect and what he is expected to do. Children generally respect rules that they make, and they learn more from rules that are positive. Rules should encourage reason and thinking and provoke active discussion. Young children typically want to please adults and be seen as "good" in their eyes. Parents should be careful to apply the right measure of discipline when rules are broken. If the parent's response is too harsh, the child may experience such a sense of shame and guilt that his initiative and sense of autonomy are affected. On the other hand, responses that are too weak could result in the child's not understanding how to control himself.

Fair and consistent rules are helpful in establishing a sense of order and control in the home. Substance-exposed children come from environments in which the out-of-control parent creates a world that is unpredictable and uncertain. In addition, the impact of exposure to alcohol and drugs on the developing fetal brain and its neurotransmitter system and neural pathways makes it difficult cognitively for the children to make the connections between cause and effect, behavior and consequence. Thus, it is critical for the foster or adoptive parent to clearly state expected behaviors with their attendant consequences. This process allows substance-affected children to develop a sense of control over their lives.

Negatively stated rules imply an expectation of misbehavior, although they tend to be easier to state than positive rules. Negatively stated rules should be avoided. Instead of saying, "Don't bring toys to the dinner table," it is just as easy to say, "We can't bring toys to the table, but we can play with them when dinner is over."

Be consistent in what is expected and in how rules are enforced. If there is a rule that a child should not interrupt his brother or sister, but then you do not enforce it when he does interrupt, inconsistency results and the power of the rule is undermined. If a child violates a rule, it should be discussed with him to make sure he understands it. Whenever possible, reminders or corrective statements for an individual child should be made in private, so as not to humiliate the child. It is important to reinforce the child for exceptional compliance with the rules by offering a special activity or reward.

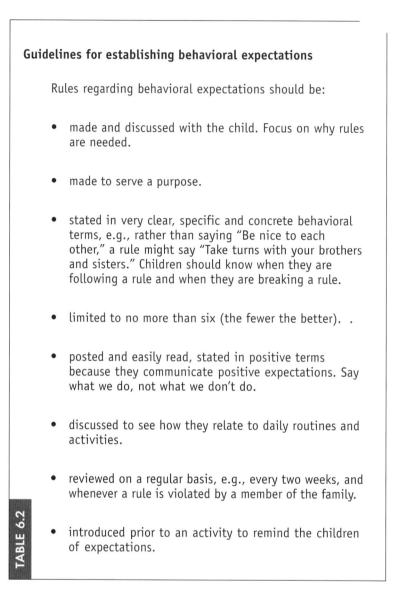

Guidelines for establishing behavioral expectations

Rules regarding behavioral expectations should be:

- made and discussed with the child. Focus on why rules are needed.

- made to serve a purpose.

- stated in very clear, specific and concrete behavioral terms, e.g., rather than saying "Be nice to each other," a rule might say "Take turns with your brothers and sisters." Children should know when they are following a rule and when they are breaking a rule.

- limited to no more than six (the fewer the better). .

- posted and easily read, stated in positive terms because they communicate positive expectations. Say what we do, not what we don't do.

- discussed to see how they relate to daily routines and activities.

- reviewed on a regular basis, e.g., every two weeks, and whenever a rule is violated by a member of the family.

- introduced prior to an activity to remind the children of expectations.

TABLE 6.2

Establishing a reward system

As a parent begins establishing a reward system, she must keep in mind that interruptions in expected rewards often cause uncertainty and confusion for younger children. If it becomes difficult to give rewards after positive behavior, then the procedures should be reviewed and revised.

To develop a reward system, first identify rewards that the child can try to earn. It is important to remember that what may be rewarding for an adult or older child may not be so for the young child. Develop a list of rewards that your child likes by asking her, observing her behavior, and talking with other parents.

Rewards should be:
- logical and natural for the home environment.
- changed and varied, with higher requirements for rewards that are more highly valued, e.g., extra play time.
- very specific, familiar and perceived to be attainable by the child.
- social as well as tangible (smiles, praise, privilege, recognition, etc.).
- given consistently for positive behavior.

At first, reinforcement should be given each time a desired behavior occurs. Plan to gradually decrease the amount of reinforcement expected. The child should be reminded why she is receiving the reward. Remember that the ultimate goal of the reward system is to try to make the social consequences strong enough to maintain a child's appropriate behavior.

Even if a tangible reward is not given each time, social rewards such as praise can be given. For younger children or children who exhibit negative behaviors often, frequency of reward for appropriate behavior is important. Minimize rewards for inappropriate or undesired behavior. Although it may seem difficult to imagine that anyone would reward undesired behavior, such events occur frequently. It is important to remember that what is rewarding for one child is not rewarding for another. For example, if a child misbehaves, the negative attention received from an adult may be rewarding for the attention-hungry child, increasing the chances for repeating the behavior.

When undesired behaviors occur, observe the reaction of the child to your response to determine if the behavior increases. If so, review your approach and consider how to respond to that child if

the situation recurs. Ignore mild occurrences of disruptive or negative behavior, if possible, which will help to reduce problems by
removing rewarding attention. Extremely disruptive or dangerous
behavior may not be able to be ignored, however, and should be
addressed.

Using social reinforcers

Children should be taught how to prompt others and provide
praise and other social reinforcers as part of group methods. Social
reinforcers are events or actions between two or more people that
serve to reinforce desired behaviors. You may wonder if a child can
be taught to provide praise and other social reinforcers to a peer.
The answer is yes. Children can be taught social reinforcement techniques, such as making positive comments, writing congratulatory
notes, giving "high five's," or dispensing stickers to each other as
rewards. Even children with attention problems can be taught to be
dispensers of reinforcement to others.

Although parents may not realize it, they use social reinforcers
frequently, such as saying "great job," "I like your effort," etc. Social
reinforcers are generally effective, but they can be even more useful for a substance-exposed child by providing detailed and specific
feedback to the child. Instead of saying, "Great job," a parent can
say, "You did a great job of paying attention and finishing your homework." Or instead of, "Great effort," say, "I could see it was hard for
you to do that math homework, but you tried really hard and got it
finished." Social reinforcers can have dramatic effects on increasing desired behavior and reducing misbehavior, especially because
children never tire of them. Further, social reinforcers are convenient because they can be given quickly, require minimal effort,
and can be used with groups or individual children.

With this understanding of the difference between external control and internal management and recognizing the parents' role in
establishing an environment for the child that is conducive to behavioral management, we will explore a variety of interventions that
can be implemented along the *SORC* continuum.

Stimulus: **Creating a consistent and predictable environment**

Children who cannot self-regulate require an environment that will help them stay below their threshold of stimulation. Swaddling a trembling, irritable drug-exposed newborn helps alleviate the infant's jitteriness by structuring the sensory environment. Structuring the physical setting for an older child and establishing a consistent and predictable environment will avoid the stimulus that sets off inappropriate behavior and will prevent the ultimate conflict that arises. Having clear expectations that are actualized will reduce the anxiety children have with ordering and organizing their own world– whether at school or at home. In fact, most of what has been written about managing the behavior of children affected by prenatal drug exposure has focused on controlling the home or school environ-

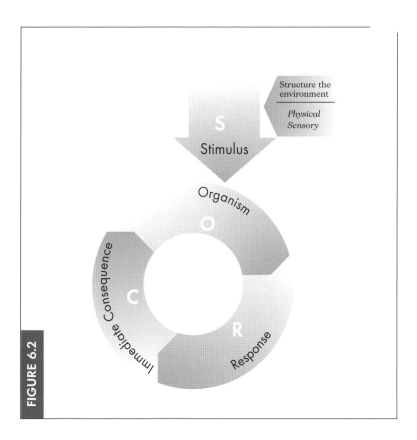

FIGURE 6.2

ment, eliminating as much as possible extraneous stimuli that will disrupt the child's learning or "set him off." This is an important first step, and frequently the easiest. But bear in mind that it will be impossible to control your child's environment as she grows and matures, so this is only a first step in the continuum. Our goal, of course, is for the child to control herself, independent of environment.

Our clinical observations lead us to believe that loss of behavioral control or withdrawal in substance-exposed children can be triggered by a number of environmental situations and stimuli. In fact, anything that increases the inconsistency and decreases the predictability of the child's environment will increase the self-regulatory problems of the child. Substance-exposed children have a hard time coping with transitions and changes in their lives. They may often display adequate regulatory abilities in familiar environments but lose this ability when presented with a new circumstance or situation.

The first step toward helping children learn to regulate is to provide them with a consistent and predictable environment. With stable routines, rules, discipline, and nurturing they know what to expect from those around them. This confidence in their environment frees them to concentrate on controlling internal states of arousal and impulses. When the children are exposed to new environments or new tasks, it is helpful to anticipate their problems and help them maintain control by providing one-on-one attention, guidance and structure.

Daily schedule

Changes to the schedule should be avoided. If the day needs to follow a different schedule, changes should be clearly explained in advance. Variations such as vacations, schedule changes, and special events can produce anxiety and distrust in children with regulatory problems. Parents should carefully assess the intended and actual value of changes for children who have difficulty in adjusting to new situations and decide if changing the child's schedule is worth the difficulties that may arise.

In the routine of daily living, parents can help their child control behavior by attending to some simple strategies:

- When the child is at home, alternate quiet and active types of activities every 20 to 30 minutes, allowing for activities that will help the child burn up energy.

- Post a daily and weekly calendar. Go over the day's schedule each morning.

- Provide closure at the end of the day. Discuss the next day and prepare for what happens tomorrow.

- If there is to be a change in the daily routine, be sure to advise the child well in advance. Something as simple as a change in car pool arrangements can disrupt the child's ability to focus and stay on task for the rest of the day.

Transitions

Transitions are times in which change is required, and can challenge even well regulated children. Transitions are usually unstructured, can be disorganized, and rarely follow a set routine. Children who need a great deal of structure or have difficulty regulating their behavior in a chaotic or less-organized situation will become lost as they move from one activity or setting to another. Routines help keep children occupied and involved and are associated with enhanced achievement.

Parents and teachers alike report that the primary time that challenging, inappropriate behaviors occur is during transition. They also have found that these behaviors decrease greatly or even are prevented if simple strategies are applied to transitions:

- Introduce the structure of transition time to the child (i.e., just like any other activity, it has a beginning, middle, and end).

- Provide clear cues or warnings to signal when a transition will soon begin, actually begin, and end (music, color codes, timers, visual cues such a lights on and off). Verbal cues are especially important: "We will leave in five minutes." "We will leave in two minutes." "We will leave in one minute." Bedtime is a particularly difficult time for many families, and these kinds of cues will help facilitate a smooth transition to sleep.

- Review the routine of a transition before it is to begin.

- Demonstrate and describe each step of a transition process for the child who requires a great deal of structured guidance.

There remains a tendency in some homes to try to get a newly arrived child to fit the typical routine, rather than fit the routine to the child. This is not to say that routines and practices that are set up for the family necessarily are inappropriate for drug-exposed children, but it may be that modifications in these procedures must be made to meet the child's unique needs.

Physical arrangement of the child's space at home

The home is the environment in which you interact with your child and where the child spends most of her time. You should provide a quiet place for the young child to re-group. The area should have minimal clutter and few toys in sight.

Unfortunately, as the child gets older, demands of homework can precipitate confrontations between parent and child. Appropriate arrangement of study space can promote study habits and prevent behavior problems. Specifically, it is important that the child's room be orderly and reassuring, providing her an opportunity to organize her behavior and her response to assigned schoolwork.

Helpful Homework Hints

- Create a "learning corner" at home to go to when your child needs to work on school assignments.

  Be sure the area is free of distractions.

Give your child a desk or table to work on his homework. Make sure the area is free of clutter, radios, and television. Use a fan or some other source of "white noise" to block out other noises around the house. Have a favorite chair or blanket nearby so that when she starts to feel overwhelmed she can get away from the cause of frustration or anxiety.

- Keep to a set schedule as much as possible.

Start homework at the same time each day and establish routines in coming home from school, enjoying some "down time," getting ready for working on the school assignments, having dinner, completing the homework. Prepare your child well in advance for any changes from that routine.

- Pay special attention to transition times.

Children with problems organizing their behavior often will have difficulty moving from one activity to another. Give your child a warning at least ten minutes ahead of time when it is time to stop working and come to dinner.

- Avoid the rush of last minute pressures.

Include long term homework assignments on your weekly calendar. Teach your child to plan and track progress toward completion of the assignment, and let her check it off when completed.

TABLE 6.3

Organism: **Organizing the thought process**

The *organism* is perhaps the least understood component in the *SORC* model. It is at the center of the continuum, through which all stimuli, responses, and consequences act. The biological changes that occur in the brain when the child is exposed prenatally to drugs or alcohol can be measured through sophisticated technology, but our understanding of the true impact of these changes on the brain's acknowledgement and interpretation of stimuli, its integration of sensory input, and its transmission of messages from the sensory to the motor cortex is far from complete. Even without a full understanding of these miracles of thought, however, we can address the organism and enhance the maturation process. For what we seek as we work with the child is to help the child make a shift from behavior that is externally controlled by stimuli to a system of internal control. Essentially, we are talking about the child's developing a locus of control from the external to the internal. This is the process of maturation.

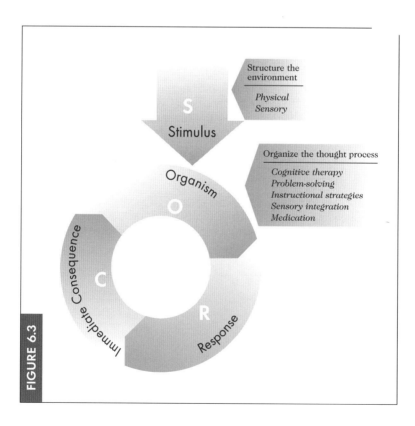

FIGURE 6.3

Teaching prosocial behavior and problem-solving

The biological and psychological background of a child who has been exposed to drugs prenatally and who may have lived her early years in a drug-seeking environment plays a key role in determining how that child will interpret and respond to stimuli. There is little adoptive parents can do about biologically based risk factors or the child's past experiences. But parents can teach a child prosocial behavior – the social and self-control skills the child will need to meet the demands encountered in school, home, and community. Teaching prosocial behavior is a combination of cognitive therapy, instructional strategies, and problem solving approaches. Although we have placed this concept of prosocial behavior within the organism component, it actually is relevant across the entire *SORC* continuum.

Developing prosocial behavior is an integral part of teaching a child behavior management that provides long-lasting effects. Substance-exposed children often have not had an opportunity to learn social skills within their home environment. Drug-abusing families do not offer feedback on behavior, or the feedback does not include what behavior would appropriately be substituted for the admonished behavior. Rules and consequences are often inconsistently administered. Children do not know what is socially appropriate and often do not know how to interact in a positive social manner. Thus the children lack the kinds of social problem-solving skills needed to guide them in making good choices as to how to behave.

Prosocial behavior can be taught through cognitive therapy but parents can take steps to teach their child prosocial behavior at home:

1. Provide opportunities for the child to have focused attention in the family conversation. Allow the child to be heard and to hear others - sharing news from school, stories from writing, work in process. This approach shapes the social situation so that it gives the child an opportunity to be reinforced for right behavior.

2. Be clear on rules and guidelines for expected ethical behaviors. Let the child participate in making rules regarding respect and inter-actions in the family.

3. Model social situations and practice interpersonal problem-solving skills that can provide positive ways for the child to assert his needs, resolve conflicts, and make friends by considering goals and developing options and their consequences. Embedding a larger repertoire of responses will serve the child well in a crisis situation.

- "If someone calls you a name, what can you do?" " If you do that, what is likely to happen?"
- "If you need something and someone is using it for a long time and won't let you use it, what can you do?" "If you do that, what is likely to happen?"
- "If someone pushes you in line...."
- "If you want someone to play with you and you are afraid to ask...."
- "If someone makes you very angry (very happy)...."

4. Model respect, friendliness, firmness of purpose and interest through interactions with the child. You can teach a child values by:

- Showing the child what you expect
- Using affirming and encouraging language
- Stressing the deed, not the doer
- Noticing and commenting on what the child does "right"
- Redirecting behavior with a firm, kind manner
- Saying what you mean, meaning what you say.

5. Provide opportunities to participate in group family activities and to learn to work together by:

- Dividing and sharing tasks
- Planning cooperative projects in the home
- Organizing group games for fun, not competition
- Assigning developmentally appropriate household chores.

6. Provide opportunities for the child to learn constructive ways to handle controversy and differences through:

- Family discussions of current events
- Suggesting different "right" solutions to the same problems
- Family meetings to discuss and solve problems
- Teaching the value of diversity and acceptance.

Instructional Strategies

Substance-exposed children who have difficulty organizing themselves within their environment often require the teacher to present an organized framework for learning. Such things as learning centers, bulletin boards, posters, and other materials can be distracting unless they have some context. This context can be provided through some simple steps to organize the classroom:

- Label classroom materials and spaces, outline their locations.
- Make neat, purposeful learning centers that are not over-stimulating and are accessible for both simple and complex materials. Use decorations that can be easily removed in case they become distracting.
- Introduce and clearly define the purpose of visual stimuli, e.g., bulletin boards, learning centers, decorations. Organize around themes.
- Define work spaces clearly and mark their boundaries.
- Provide private areas and soft elements such as pillows and rugs, rocking chairs, and headphones.
- Give each student a space for his/her belongings.
- Clearly identify and mark materials. Keep clutter to a minimum.
- Limit distractions and ensure adequate light and ventilation.
- Within the context of this overall strategy, provide a quiet, "calm down," or "alone" space where children can go to regain their organization, balance, and self-control.

In presenting new material or giving instructions to the students, the teacher should organize her approach in a step-wise manner.

Students can become overloaded easily if too much information is provided at once. Information can be processed much more successfully by the child with regulatory problems if guidance is provided in clear, discrete steps that build upon each other.

Sensory integration

Since the late 1980's, sensory integration therapy has been recognized as an important component of therapy for alcohol- and drug-exposed children. Sensory integration is a dynamic neurological process. It is the capacity of the central nervous system to integrate information from the various senses to enable the person to interact with the world. Sensory integration therapy focuses on the neurologic process that organizes sensations from the body. The goal of therapy is to help the child process and integrate multiple streams of sensory information. Its use with substance-exposed children has been especially beneficial in helping children recognize and interpret stimuli appropriately. Although sensory integration therapy requires the skills of a specially trained occupational therapist to be fully implemented, parents should be aware of its usefulness and seek consultation when appropriate.

Medication

As discussed previously, it can be difficult to differentiate behavioral difficulties due to prenatal drug or alcohol exposure from Attention Deficit Hyperactivity Disorder (ADHD). In fact, the common neurochemical changes that occur in the brain in both clinical situations are almost identical. That is why the most common question that arises in working with prenatally exposed children is whether the child should be placed on medication. Unfortunately, the use of stimulant medications, such as Ritalin, has become a reflexive action on the part of many physicians, and large numbers of children with behavioral problems are placed on medication without a thorough evaluation. As of the year 2000, more than two million children in the United States were taking Ritalin or a similar drug.

Children often are diagnosed with ADHD when actually they have other problems that mimic its symptoms. This problem arises because the diagnostic criteria for ADHD (inability to sustain attention and concentration in more than one setting, developmentally inappropriate levels of activity, distractibility, and impulsivity) are not strictly followed. Some rambunctious children get the label of ADHD when their parents think Ritalin will make the children behave. On the other side of the coin, many children, especially among black and Hispanic populations, do not receive appropriate medication when in fact it would help them. Finally, Ritalin often is used incorrectly as a diagnostic tool. "Let's put him on Ritalin and see what happens." An improvement in the child's behavior is then wrongly interpreted as evidence of ADHD.

If Ritalin or another medication is suggested for a child, parents should be aware of some key issues:

- Disorders that have symptoms very much like ADHD, such as depression, anxiety, schizophrenia and learning problems, often are misdiagnosed as ADHD. This can cause a great deal of harm from both the physiological and psychological perspective. Obviously, the primary problem must be addressed, and giving a child Ritalin or another stimulant medication can only make things worse.

- Inappropriate behavioral or learning expectations can redefine normal behavior as abnormal. This has become an especially significant problem as school systems across the country have established mandatory learning standards in the last few years. This has led to frustration and alienation in students who have trouble measuring up.

- Managed health care insurance companies save money on psychiatric or psychological evaluations by relying on primary care doctors to diagnose ADHD and prescribe Ritalin. Parents must insist on a comprehensive evaluation by a team of physicians and psychologists who have thorough knowledge of ADHD and other behavioral difficulties that mimic ADHD.

Even with these constraints, it is important for parents to realize that medications do help many children, especially if they have behavioral difficulties related to prenatal drug or alcohol exposure. And, contrary to popular thought, the use of medications for behavioral problems does not put a child at increased risk for drug abuse or addiction later in life. In fact, a recent study showed that the children with the greatest risk of developing addiction problems in adolescence were those that needed medication and did not receive it. The bottom line is that medication has a role in helping address the behavioral and learning difficulties that prenatally exposed children may suffer, but placing a child on medication requires thought and is only one component in a comprehensive intervention plan.

Response: Identifying and replacing inappropriate behavior

Children are not simple, and they usually present a range of behaviors that challenge parents rather than a couple of clearly defined behaviors. Most common is the child who is experienced as "difficult about everything." Problems often include a combination of academic failure, inability to complete work, oppositional behavior, and bad temper. Such a child is likely to be described as "difficult," "challenging," or "impossible," but often will be hard to describe in exact "observables." Thus, the first step in trying to change a child's behavioral response is to identify the behavior that needs to be changed. It is important to identify the target behavior specifically and in observable ways. There is no way to define interventions that will make a child less difficult or challenging, but we can talk about how to help a child be more compliant, be more able to complete his schoolwork, and not hit others when he is frustrated or angry.

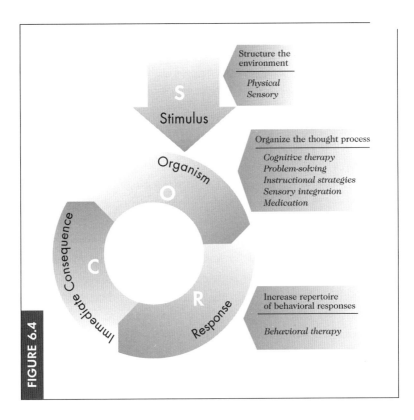

FIGURE 6.4

Structure the environment

Physical
Sensory

Stimulus

Organize the thought process

Cognitive therapy
Problem-solving
Instructional strategies
Sensory integration
Medication

Organism

Increase repertoire of behavioral responses

Behavioral therapy

Response

Consequence

Immediate

Identifying a target behavior

In a family setting, there are frequent disruptions that are isolated in nature and can be dealt with on the spot. Sometimes the situation is very clear, such as when a child who is not typically aggressive is provoked into hitting by a highly confrontational child.

However, when this type of behavior is repeated, it is likely to be identified as a target behavior.

Identification of a target behavior can be guided by a series of questions:

1. Can you specifically name the behavior and document how often it occurs or how long it continues?

2. Can you describe the behavior to teachers or other parents so they know exactly what you mean (e.g., "Does not finish dinner.")? If someone asks you what you mean, it may indicate you are not yet specific enough. Even in this example, you might need to add, "Does not finish dinner in the allotted time."

3. Does the child understand what you are asking him to do?

4. If a teacher or other parent were to observe the child or behavior in question, would she agree about the behavior and its severity?

The specificity elicited by answering these kinds of questions will be critical as you try to address the child's behavioral difficulties. You will find yourself getting "stuck" in the process if you have not carefully defined the specific behaviors that are problematic. If this happens, you may need to further clarify the specific behaviors or difficulties the child is presenting. If you have trouble specifying those behaviors, you might try sitting down with your spouse or other parents and having them ask you questions about the problems until they begin to take more specific form.

CASE STUDY: Cheryl

■ You find Cheryl's behavior to be generally annoying. Among the things you find annoying is that Cheryl talks continually and is constantly interrupting you and her siblings. What behavior do you want to target?

Case discussion

You can't target "annoying" without specifying it more clearly. The target behavior has to be specific and observable, and it must occur repeatedly over a period of time. Based on the information above, you would target Cheryl's frequent talking and constant interruptions.

■ ■

Providing a repertoire of responses to replace the target behavior

Most behaviors serve a function for the child; thus, it is very difficult to eliminate the behavior or to change it without providing the child with a substitute behavior that can serve the same function. This does not mean you cannot have clear rules about the unacceptability of certain behaviors. Some rules are not negotiable, and some behaviors are simply not acceptable under any circumstance. You should state these few prohibitions emphatically: "You may not hit another child," "You may not destroy other people's property," or "You may not put other people in danger." Such rules should be limited in number and stated in clear, unequivocal ways. Children often benefit from regular discussion of these guidelines, and frequent reminders are critical: "What are the important rules?" "Why do we have these rules?"

Because most behavior is functional, efforts to change it without substitution usually are unsuccessful or only temporarily helpful. Aggressive behavior is a normal response to frustration. Think about your own response when you feel very frustrated and you'd like to yell, slam a door, or hit the first thing available. Think about the state of tension and stress you feel and the release you experience if you can take it out in some act of aggression. As an adult, you have developed other ways of managing this state of tension, but it often takes very little to overwhelm children with low tolerance for frustration, resulting in an aggressive behavioral response. Frustration can result when the child is asked to do something he doesn't want to do ("a demand"), including stopping an activity to transition to another. Schoolwork that is "too difficult," other children taking control, being teased, being punished — all of these situations can result in a state of tension to which the child responds through aggressive behavior.

Children who come from a family situation in which they have been chronically ignored often have learned the best way to get attention is through negative behavior. Sometimes these behaviors also may be an effort to gain control. While adults tend to feel manipulated by these behaviors, it is more helpful in the problem-solving process to realize the function of such manipulative, attention-seeking behaviors. What kinds of behaviors are you ready to provide attention to? How much control are you willing to give a child if she acts appropriately?

Once you discern the function of a behavior, there are many tools at your disposal. You can look at the behavior in context and identify another behavior that is functionally the same but incompatible with the difficult or inappropriate behavior (e.g., relaxation is incompatible with arousal). However, you must be sure that you have targeted a specific behavior to address and know what replacement behavior you want to instill in the child before beginning to intervene.

What can we offer the child as a substitute for aggression when the state of tension is too high? You can't make a child stop feeling angry, but you can substitute what constitutes angry behavior. In fact, just validating the feeling along with setting a limit can be a very powerful intervention. For example, you may say, "Derrick, I see that you are feeling very angry, but we cannot hit our friends." Feeling understood and validated often has a calming effect on children (and adults, too).

It is important for the parent to realize that relaxation is incompatible with arousal, so if you can help a child reduce arousal through relaxation, the other more disruptive behaviors that discharge the arousal state are no longer needed. Some suggestions for the child to help manage his frustration include those that most adults use: relaxing the tension internally by removing oneself from the situation and "talking oneself down" to a calm state, using visualization to imagine a favorite haunt or activity, counting to ten, closing one's eyes, taking a deep breath and letting it out slowly, listening to calming music, or going alone to a place that is soothing. You can help children do these things when they are frustrated. You also can help them to reduce the impulsivity that usually accompanies these behaviors. For example, you may want to provide a punching pillow or stomping pad where a child can go when he wants to hurt another child by acting aggressively. By the time the child has left the situation to go to the stomping corner, he has controlled his impulse, and the stomping serves only to release the residual tension.

CASE STUDY: *Tawanda*

▐ Tawanda talks in class and bothers other students, especially when she is working on math, which is her most difficult subject area. Her interruptions occur when she gets excited or when attention is directed away from her. Thus, talking seems to be her way of responding to anxiety, excitement and lack of attention. Based on these ideas, what replacement behaviors might you consider?

Case discussion

Tawanda's immediate response to the frustration she feels when working on math problems is to find a way in which she can discharge the high levels of energy she is experiencing. As a replacement behavior, Tawanda should give a cue to the teacher that she needs extra help or the teacher should pair Tawanda with another child for whom math is an area of strength.

CASE STUDY: *Chris*

▐ Chris becomes upset and disruptive when lining up to go to lunch or to change classes. Fire drills particularly send him off task, and he has trouble "keeping his hands to himself" for the rest of the day. What function could Chris' noisy and disobedient behavior be serving?

Case discussion

Chris is discharging excess tension and the over-stimulation he feels when there is a change in the schedule by becoming noisy and disobedient. He especially seems to have difficulty structuring his own behavior when there is not a clear, externally imposed structure. He then gets excited and has trouble calming down. Thus the behaviors that are problematic serve as Chris' best efforts to regulate and structure himself. You consider other ways Chris may be able to regulate himself, such as relaxation, developing a capacity to problem-solve and structure for himself, and learning calming strategies.

The most important aspect of reading and responding to messages is the basic but critical ability to be empathic. This means successfully picking up on the message embedded in behaviors, and responding with empathy to that message and the function it is serving. Empathic, reflective statements such as, "I see that you're angry about this," or "It seems like you're having trouble organizing this work by yourself," or "I know it was easy to be distracted by your sister's telephone call, but now let's see if we can focus on the work and remember what we need to do," can be very powerful interventions in and of themselves, as they allow a child to feel understood, enhancing his sense of trust and safety with that adult.

However, on an every day basis, a parent can reach the point where she feels unable to deal with the problems facing her. It is hard to feel empathy when you feel powerless. So the parent responds out of her own frustration. Empowerment is the degree to which the parent feels capable of dealing with the child's behavior, including the problems arising from negative or disruptive behavior. Parents who feel empowered are more likely to engage in problem solving and respond in empathic, proactive ways, while those who do not feel empowered may feel frustrated and angry, and react without reflection, thinking there is no solution to the problem.

■ ■

Consequences: Making sense for the child

When attempts to manage behavior are rooted in punitive or negative approaches, it is very possible that behavioral problems will increase as the child retaliates. In the *SORC* model of understanding behavior, we know that the immediate consequence of the child's behavioral response tends to be the one that guides future behavior.

Any event that follows a behavioral response is a consequence, whether it is reinforcement or punishment. However, punishment, especially positive punishment, is unpredictable and often counterproductive when working with drug-exposed children. On the other hand, if a consequence is logical, it helps the child look more closely at her behavior and think about the results of her choices. "Logical consequences" do not punish or reward, but instill responsibility for

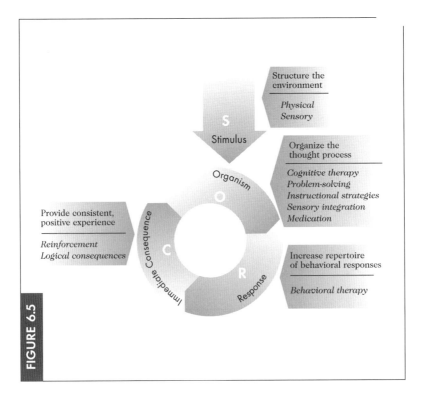

FIGURE 6.5

choices and actions in children. While rules help guide children to construct their environment in a safe and orderly fashion, logical consequences reinforce cause and effect thinking and allow children to internalize strategies of self-control and commitment.

Another key concept to remember as reinforcement and punishment are considered is the contingency, or connection, between an immediate consequence (such as a positive reinforcement) and the appropriate behavior. Receiving a positive reinforcement is contingent (dependent) upon the child's performing the appropriate behavior. Understanding this contingency relationship and the difference between a contingency and an immediate consequence will be important when you develop interventions. Children should not be given consequences unless they know what to expect and can make the choice to control their behavior appropriately. Then the consequence becomes a contingency because the child is put in the position of understanding the dependent relationship between his behavior and the reinforcement or punishment.

CASE STUDY: Jake

■ Jake stops doing his homework and begins teasing his sister. His father tells him to stop. Jake continues to tease her. His father again says, "Stop teasing your sister." Jake ignores his father's request. Finally, Jake's father says, "I've had enough; go to your room!"

Case discussion

Jake's immediate consequence for teasing his sister is a release of negative tension he has built up around the frustration he feels about his homework. Jake's father's reaction to Jake's teasing also is an immediate consequence of his behavior, but not a contingency. Had his father said the first time, "Jake, if you continue to tease your sister I will send you to your room," he would have set up the contingency and given Jake a chance to make a choice and take responsibility for his own behavior. If you use a consequence without setting it up as a contingency, you lose the power of the contingency because you have not allowed the child to make the choice of what he will do. Establishing contingencies is especially important for drug-exposed children because it empowers them to make choices about, and thus learn to regulate, their own behavior.

■ ■

Utilizing contingencies and logical consequences

Although reward systems may help to promote positive behavior, parents often must move to more active approaches to minimize undesired behaviors. The use of contingencies and logical consequences is successful in children as they reach school age.

Contingencies are a central concept to effective behavior management, although their meaning may be unclear. The best synonym for the term is "dependent" and refers to the relationship of one event to another. If there is a contingent relationship between two events, then one is a result of (i.e., dependent upon) the occurrence of the other. For example, an adult receiving a paycheck is contingent (dependent) upon her working. A child receives an "A" grade contingent upon doing the necessary work. A child receives a reward contingent upon whether she completes a task for which a reward has been promised.

Many parents are uncomfortable with the idea of using rewards to help children manage their behavior, equating the use of such a contingency to that of a bribe. But using such incentives or consequences are very powerful interventions that provide the message: "You (the child) are in charge of what happens, I am not controlling you — it's up to you." Thus, the parent, rather than being the punitive provider of punishments, becomes the coach who can empower the child to see that he can exert control and manage himself. Positive incentives are an especially useful tool with children who are oppositional and defiant. Incentives are also a way to acknowledge that you are asking a child to do something that is difficult for her. It is no different from the kinds of incentives and bonuses provided to adults in the workplace when employers want more productivity, e.g., the promise of a promotion or raise. Incentives motivate and give the individual, adult or child, control over the decision-making process. When you offer an incentive for successful execution of something that you understand requires much effort, you are providing an empathic intervention that lets a child know you understand him and do not blame him if he cannot complete the task.

Incentives and contingencies also help children who tend to be impulsive by helping them think before they act. If the wish to act (i.e., hit another child) and the action itself are essentially simultaneous, the child is not in a position to make a different choice (i.e., walk away). Incentives help a child put a couple of beats between the wish to act and the action (i.e., "If I hit this kid, I'll lose my sticker"), and thus help build her capacity for self-control by having successful experiences.

Using these types of interventions also allows the parent to be very creative and involved with his child. What motivates the child? How can the contingency be structured? How can the child work to meet extra goals? But remember, the chosen contingency must be meaningful to the child — that is, it must be something she wants, so it will provide the motivation and incentive she needs to reach the targeted goal.

There are many examples of establishing contingencies or relationships in managing behavior. In fact, the large majority of every-day behavior is a product of the contingencies established among events or objects. We all receive rewards or positive consequences as a function of our behavior, e.g., a "thank you" for helping someone with a problem. We can also receive negative consequences for inappropriate behavior, e.g., receiving a traffic ticket for speeding. Obviously then, not all contingencies support adaptive behavior. A child can get attention for misbehavior. For example, a child who acts aggressively may get attention from a subset of his peers. Thus, getting the attention is contingent upon being aggressive. A contingency by itself is neither positive nor negative, but it is the nature of the relationship that is important.

The idea of contingencies also can be viewed as logical consequences when teaching children to take responsibility for their own behavior. This notion of logical consequences is most effective with drug-exposed children because it reinforces the idea of self-regulation and puts children in charge of themselves by encouraging them to examine their own behaviors and think about the choices they make. By doing so they are able to regain their self-control and their self-respect.

CASE STUDY: *Ronnie*

■ Ronnie is a third-grader who has difficulty completing all his homework due to visual-motor difficulties as well as attentional deficits that make it hard for him to copy the ten sentences from the paper assigned by the teacher. This results in power struggles at home, with Ronnie usually going to bed feeling defeated and angry and his parents feeling frustrated. Despite suggestions by the learning

Guidelines for Logical Consequences

- Logical consequences are respectful of the child and the family. The child gives input into possible consequences including choices about specifics of consequences. Logical consequences are not intended to humiliate or hurt.

- Logical consequences need to respond to choices and actions, not character. The message is that misbehavior results from poor judgment or bad planning but not from poor character.

- Logical consequences need to be put into practice with both empathy and *structure*. Empathy shows our knowledge of children and our willingness to hear what they have to say; structure establishes and provides appropriate directions. The parent needs to be firm and kind. Kindness shows respect for the child; firmness shows respect for oneself.

- Logical consequences should be used to describe the demands of the situation, not the demands of the authority. This helps avoid power struggles.

- Logical consequences should be used only after the parent has assessed the situation. Misbehavior may result from expectations that are not appropriate to the developmental needs of the child, or from expectations incompatible with the child's particular needs. The best alternative may be to restructure the environment and readjust the expectations. When confronted with misbehavior, there are two questions to ask:
    a) Are my expectations appropriate to the age needs of the child?
    b) Are my expectations appropriate to the individual needs and abilities of the child?

- Stop and think before imposing logical consequences. We all often need time to think, not just to react.

- Logical consequences help to restore self-control and self-respect because self-respect demands not just words, but actions.

TABLE 6.4

disabilities teacher and an outside psychologist, Ronnie's teacher refuses to modify the number of sentences Ronnie has to copy in order to receive credit for completion. Ronnie displays considerable disruptive behavior at school and is becoming more difficult to manage.

Case discussion

This teacher has a clearly defined policy that no child can be exempted from the expected work in her classroom, as this would undermine her authority. But the distant consequence of "not receiving credit" has no logical connection for Ronnie. What do the teacher and Ronnie gain from this rule? Ronnie still does not complete his assignment, undermining his sense of competence and making him angrier and more frustrated, leading to behavioral problems that require the teacher's attention and energy. The teacher becomes angry because she has to focus so much time on Ronnie.

If, on the other hand, the teacher would consider reducing Ronnie's assignment, Ronnie will be successful both in completing the assignment and in managing himself. The teacher will be able to give him positive feedback and not have to engage in more intrusive behavior management techniques. It can be seen that, despite the wish to use rules equally for all students, the logical consequences of those rules can have results that clearly undermine the success of both the child and the classroom.

Logical consequences bring the entire *SORC* model together. The child understands that, "This is what happened, this is the way I feel, this is the consequence of what I did." When the child reaches this point, the organism begins to mature; the child's sense of self-efficacy grows. He knows what starts it and knows where it leads. "If I chill out, I will avoid that situation."

CHAPTER

The Problem-Solving Process for Behavior Management

Disorders of regulation, attention and arousal are not cured but must be managed throughout childhood. Parenting support and academic instruction that help children learn to process information and to plan, monitor, revise, and evaluate an approach to complete a task allows children who often feel out of control to take control of their own learning process. Educators and psychologists agree that this ability is crucial to learning and success in cognitive development and academic achievement.

A child's misbehavior can create chaos for a family, and parents often fear that the time and energy they devote to working with a child with behavioral problems will result in their neglecting their other children. The guilt, disappointment, and frustration that come with every new incident can cloud the best intentions of even the most caring mothers and fathers, and they often find themselves reacting to a situation rather than thinking it through. In these circumstances, a structured and systematic approach to behavior management is needed.

Utilizing the key concepts described in the *SORC* model and relying on positive reinforcement and logical consequences, we will build on our understanding of behavioral regulation difficulties in the drug-exposed child and develop a structured problem-solving process for behavior management. It should be noted that although we have been discussing the SORC model in a linear fashion, our actual problem-solving process will address interventions at multiple and varied points along the SORC continuum.

If you think about the way you relate to your child, you will realize that most of your interventions focus on the "organism" through insight learning. That is, you tell a child something once, and you expect him to have the insight to remember it and apply it in a variety of situations. However, many prenatally exposed children do not have the benefit of insight learning. This goes back to our previous discussion of the impact of alcohol and other drugs on the fetal brain and the development of the dopamine receptor system and the neural pathways. So as a parent, you frequently will experience one step forward and one step back. "He gets it, then he forgets it."

Using the problem-solving process helps maintain an objective, systematic approach to behavioral interventions. It involves the process of monitoring the child's behavior, adapting interventions to the individual style and needs of both the parent and the child, evaluating the success or failure of the joint efforts, and then revising the intervention strategy accordingly. But the most important aspect of the problem-solving process is to understand the child and his behavior and then to identify the appropriate point of entry into the *SORC* model.

As you study the problem-solving process, you will realize that the various components of *SORC* come into play. Steps 1 and 2 are an observation of the child's behavioral response *(R)*. Step 3 considers stimuli *(S)* that may be initiating the behavioral response and characteristics of the organism *(O)* that have a role in interpreting the stimuli. Steps 4 and 5 expand the child's repertoire of behavioral responses *(R)* to replace the inappropriate behavior. Step 6 directly addresses the child *(O)* to help him at a cognitive level begin to internalize his ability to control his own behavior, and Step 7 addresses immediate consequences to reinforce and maintain appropriate behavior. Step 8 brings the *SORC* continuum together, evaluating the impact of your intervention.

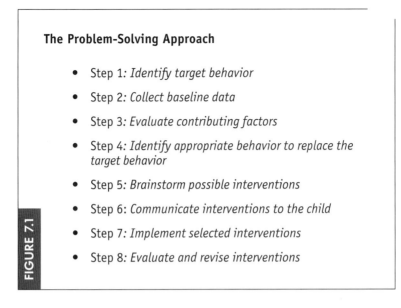

The Problem-Solving Approach

- Step 1: *Identify target behavior*
- Step 2: *Collect baseline data*
- Step 3: *Evaluate contributing factors*
- Step 4: *Identify appropriate behavior to replace the target behavior*
- Step 5: *Brainstorm possible interventions*
- Step 6: *Communicate interventions to the child*
- Step 7: *Implement selected interventions*
- Step 8: *Evaluate and revise interventions*

FIGURE 7.1

Step 1: Identify the target behavior

Identification of a target behavior can be guided by a series of questions:

1. Can you specifically name the behavior and document how often it occurs or how long it continues?

2. Can you describe the behavior to teachers or other parents so they know exactly what you mean (e.g., "Does not finish dinner.")? If someone asks you what you mean, it may indicate you are not yet specific enough. Even in this example, you might need to add, "Does not finish dinner in the allotted time."

3. Does the child understand what you are asking him to do?

4. If a teacher or other parent were to observe the child or behavior in question, would she agree about the behavior and its severity?

Step 2: Collect baseline data

Now that you have specified those behaviors you think you want to change or modify, you need to collect baseline data about them. The term "baseline" refers to initial levels of behavior before intervention; that is, you want to objectively examine the extent of the behaviors you have identified as problematic. This process allows you to record behavior in an impartial manner and thus gives you a measured way of checking your subjective reactions. All adults have a wide range of attitudes and responses to certain situations. Foster and adoptive parents and teachers can be affected by any number of things, including the way a child looks, the child's family background, how much the child is liked, the child's personality and attitudes, and experiences with the child's biologic parents. Baseline data answer the question, "Do I really see what I think I see?"

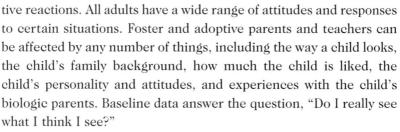

Collecting baseline data allows you to observe behaviors and determine their severity in the context of the situation. In some cases, the behaviors may occur inconsistently or sporadically, making it difficult to determine the actual severity of the behavior. Often in this case you may see that the intervention should be immediate and will not require a long-term, individual problem-solving process. Once you have established that a behavior occurs with enough frequency to warrant a more elaborate intervention, you will need to establish the context in which the behavior occurs. Collecting "baseline" data is not only about the child's behavior, but also about what is happening in the classroom when the behavior occurs. The context and conditions in which the behavior occurs are critical to selecting a successful strategy.

From an evaluation perspective, determining the extent of a problem by collecting baseline data allows you to determine whether an intervention has had any effect. After you have implemented the chosen intervention strategy and given it a chance to have an impact on the child, you will want to recollect data on the behaviors targeted. If you collected good baseline data before you started, then you will be able to compare your before and after numbers and determine whether your interventions modified the targeted behaviors and, if so, by how much. This is valuable information to guide future intervention strategies as new problems develop.

How might you go about collecting baseline data on behavior? First, remember the specific behaviors you are interested in, then create a chart that lists those behaviors. Begin to observe the child carefully to get a sense about those behaviors you want to target and to help you establish objective criteria.

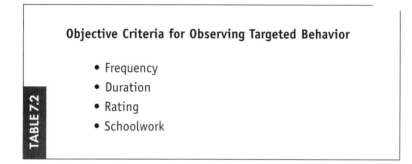

Objective Criteria for Observing Targeted Behavior

TABLE 7.2

- Frequency
- Duration
- Rating
- Schoolwork

Frequency of behavior

You can establish baseline frequency just by keeping track of how often the targeted inappropriate behavior occurs within a specific time period; for example, how often is the child off-task during a one-hour period of independently doing his homework? You can determine the frequency of a behavior by counting all the occurrences of the behavior during a selected time period (hour, day, or week), or by taking a sample during each of several different time periods. For example, rather than counting the total number of times the child hits his sister during a three hour period, you could observe the child's behavior for two or three minutes at several different times. This method of sampling, if done well, will give a good approximation of the frequency of behavior without diverting too much of your time from other matters. When evaluating frequency of behavior, be sure the behavior is not being caused by something unusual in the child's environment, such as the unexpected arrival of a guest or other children visiting the child's brothers and sisters. You can use any convenient system to gather frequency data, such as putting tally marks on a sheet of paper where you have noted the targeted behaviors, using note cards, or any other method that you might improvise.

Duration of behavior

Another way to establish baseline information is to assess how long a behavior lasts. Rather than counting the number of times a child is off-task while doing homework, determine how long the child is off-task within a given period. If the child is off-task for three minutes out of five, then the duration of the inappropriate behavior is 60% for that period. You can take several samples to verify that off-task behavior is occurring during other time periods and under a variety of circumstances. Duration recording is useful when behaviors are more continuous rather than behaviors that occur intermittently, such as staring out the window or not working independently.

Ratings of behavior

There are several standardized scales that can be used to rate the severity of a child's behaviors. The results represent the parent's composite impression of a child's behavior over time. Most psychologists are familiar with these scales. You can consult with your school's psychologist to determine what scales are available and might be useful to you or you can devise your own criteria with as simple an approach as mild, moderate and severe.

Evaluation of work

Depending on the nature of the targeted behavior, the child's current performance on schoolwork also may be helpful in collecting baseline information. Records of the number of tasks or problems attempted, the number completed, and the accuracy (e.g., percent correct on each assignment) can provide you with effective baseline data upon which to base an intervention for a behavior that interferes with completion of academic work. Letter grades are not adequate because they tend to be subjective. In addition, grades are not sensitive enough to show short-term changes. The child may make progress, but this will not be reflected in a change of grade until the progress continues consistently over a long period of time. This is inadequate for purposes of evaluating the impact of your chosen intervention. For this reason, schoolwork itself rather than a grade is a more useful source of baseline data.

The need to be objective when collecting these kinds of data is critical because behavior and the perception of its severity are always affected by an individual's subjective experience and expectations. What is considered disruptive or inappropriate in one environment may be viewed very differently in another. Each parent brings to his child-rearing approach his own tolerance level, expectations for children's behavior, and preferences for some types of children over others. There has been a tendency in the past to label drug-exposed children as "uncontrollable," which clearly is not true. However, it is easy for perceptions to be confused with reality and for children, especially those from troubled families, to be blamed for problems that actually reflect skill deficits.

In addition to using the strategies discussed above to establish a baseline, you also need to note when the behaviors occur in order to put them into context. Think about the behaviors you've noted: Do they occur first thing in the morning, after school, at the end of the day, right before lunch? What tends to trigger the targeted behaviors (an interruption in the daily routine, another child in the family getting into trouble, the mother working with another child)? Can you begin to predict when you will be most likely to see the targeted behaviors and, if so, what is the context in which they occur? By understanding a behavior within the context of the environment, you may find that something at home is actually contributing to the problem. Perhaps you notice that each time Adam is off-task while doing his homework, he is looking at the constantly moving model airplane hanging nearby. Adam may in fact be off-task because of a distraction in the room that was created by the parent.

CASE STUDY: Tawanda

You have decided to target Tawanda's talking behavior and interruptions. You hope to determine if these behaviors are the source of your irritation with her. What would you do to determine that your belief is actually supported by fact and is not influenced by your own bias caused by your general feeling of annoyance with this child?

Case Discussion

Pure numerical data would help support or dispel your perception. Counting the frequency of Tawanda's interruptions (i.e., how many interruptions occur in various one-hour periods) would provide an objective view of how often she interrupts conversations. To create a baseline of her talking behavior, you may decide to record the percentage of minutes she talks and interrupts during family dinnertime. It would be critical to include observations that tell you the circumstances when this talking occurs.

--- **CASE STUDY: Chris**

■ Now that you have decided that the target behaviors include those that indicate Chris is overly excited and is having trouble calming down, you can set up a behavior log to determine what kind of behaviors are exhibited and at what times. Establish a log that allows you to record Chris' behavior each time you have to discipline him. Note what activity is occurring at this moment and exactly what Chris is doing. You may also want to note what you did in response to his behavior and whether it had a positive impact. You should collect the data for at least a week.

■ ■

Step 3: Evaluate contributing factors

The problem-solving process involves consideration of factors that may contribute to the inappropriate behaviors you have targeted. Contributing factors are either "direct" — that is, those factors that have a direct and close relationship to current problems, or "indirect" — those that indirectly contribute to current problems.

Direct factors

Direct factors influence the child's behavior directly at the level of the organism (developmental status, learning disabilities, skill deficits, medical problems, emotional or psychological problems, poor frustration tolerance, low tolerance for stimulation) or as a stimulus (the home's physical environment, family events, or a noisy classroom).

Indirect factors

Indirect factors usually cannot be changed in the foster or adoptive home because they were associated with the child's biologic family history. Clearly, little or nothing can be done about the fact that a child was abused or neglected before coming to his adoptive home, but this is an important part of understanding the function and meaning of the child's behavior.

Most often direct and indirect factors come together and contribute to current behavioral problems, but you may be able to improve behavior by modifying their effects. For example, suppose a child with emotional problems tends to withdraw when criticized. The child may have a history of being severely criticized and may have learned to withdraw as a way to cope with the criticism. The indirect contributing factor is how the child has been treated, which you cannot change. However, the direct contributing factor is how the child reacts to criticism. You can approach the child in such a way as to reduce his tendency to withdraw and increase his participation in his new family's life.

The first step in evaluating contributing factors is to gather information from observations of the child. Since you've collected baseline data, you may already have some ideas about when the problem behavior occurs, which will allow you to hypothesize about what is going on. Perhaps you've noticed that Craig's off-task, disruptive talking occurs whenever you are talking to the family in general without any visual cues or stimulation. Perhaps this child has difficulty with auditory processing and needs visual information to help him stay on track. Or in tracking impulsive-aggressive behavior, you've noticed that Daniel acts out after he's been unable to successfully complete his homework, suggesting low tolerance for frustration as a key to his behavior. Sallie's behavior is fine during the morning, but in the afternoon she can't stop talking, constantly moves around and doesn't comply with limits. You notice this is less true on days when the weather is inclement and she cannot go outside to play. You begin to notice Randall is unable to settle down after active, unstructured play and he has a general deficit with structuring or organizing himself in less structured situations.

Fully understanding all the factors that contribute to your child's behavior will require an open conversation with your child. First, always consider immediate factors in the child's life (recent move into a new foster home, family illness, death, changes in household composition) to help put the child's behavior in context and allow you to choose an informed solution to the problem. Evaluate these factors in a nonjudgmental and respectful manner and talk with your child in a calm, nonthreatening manner. Through this conversation you may learn of indirect factors bothering the child that were not immediately apparent to you.

For example, Denisha's behavior is highly variable and changes from day to day. You will want to explore whether she has noticed that she has some good days and some more difficult ones, and see if she has any ideas about the contrast. You might learn that some nights Denisha doesn't sleep well, and that she can't manage herself the next day. Or you might find out that in her biologic home, on some mornings Denisha was on her own because of her mother's sporadic work schedule. Denisha was angry and overwhelmed by this situation. Or you may learn that Denisha's father was in and out of the home and that when he was around there were incidents of violence that upset Denisha. Knowledge of any of these problems will help you understand the behavior you are seeing and guide you in planning ways to help the child.

Establish contributing factors

Once you have documented a behavior and established the context in which the behavior occurs, you can begin to think in terms of the function of the behavior and move to the next phase in the problem-solving process.

CASE STUDY: Tawanda

■ You have collected baseline data on the frequency of Tawanda's interruptions at home and you have talked with her teacher to document the amount of time she spends talking at various points in the school day. You have recorded a range of observations about the situations in which these behaviors occur. What contributing factors might be influencing Tawanda's behavior?

Case Discussion

In evaluating the baseline data you can see that at home, Tawanda most frequently interrupts you when you are on the telephone, putting Tawanda's younger sibling to bed or you are involved in some other important activity. You talk to Tawanda's teacher and learn that Tawanda talks more often at school during math class than other subject areas, disturbing the work of other children by trying to see their work or asking them questions. Interruptions, including Tawanda's getting out of her seat, occur most frequently when the teacher is working with another student and when, during a class discussion, she calls on another student. Tawanda's talking increases during field trips, assembly programs and similar events in which there is a lot of activity and excitement.

CASE STUDY: Chris

■ By collecting baseline data, you have been able to verify your perception that Chris has trouble managing himself whenever structure in the home is reduced, especially when moving through transitions from one activity to another and when given free time to play. Under these circumstances, Chris becomes overly excited, exhibits poor self-control, and has trouble calming down. What are the contributing factors that may affect Chris' transition problems?

You go to school and talk with Chris' kindergarten teacher, who confirms Chris' difficulty with transitions, saying he does not like changes of any sort and gets "wild." As a younger child, changes in routine and being in situations that were highly stimulating were very difficult for Chris to manage. Chris' baseline information indicated that he was slow to change from one activity to another: he was not ready for the new activity 50% of the time. Chris also appeared to have difficulty when his "space" was invaded (in the back seat of the car, in a line at school, in the elevator during a field trip). He became overexcited and aggressive in these situations and ignored requests to quiet down 70% of the time.

■ ■

Step 4: Identify appropriate behavior to replace the target behavior

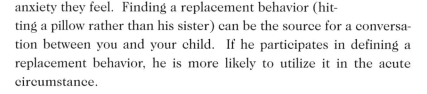

As discussed in previous chapters, there is a reason for all behaviors, and you cannot take away one behavior without giving the child options for other behaviors to replace it. Children must have the opportunity to release the tension and anxiety they feel. Finding a replacement behavior (hitting a pillow rather than his sister) can be the source for a conversation between you and your child. If he participates in defining a replacement behavior, he is more likely to utilize it in the acute circumstance.

Step 5: Brainstorm possible interventions

Develop a list of possible interventions. Your primary goal as you consider various interventions is to decide what you can do at home and in the routine of family living that will stack the deck in your child's favor. Think of child-proofing your home when your children were young. You covered electrical outlets, you locked cabinets, you stored harmful cleaning solutions on high shelves. You took a prevention approach to protect your child's physical health. Now you must use prevention strategies to protect your child's emotional health.

Examine the possible interventions

After brainstorming a variety of interventions, explore the positives and negatives of each of the possible approaches. Give each intervention serious consideration, then select the intervention that would be the least intrusive yet makes the most sense. To determine which intervention you will select you should consider the potential for effectiveness, the acceptability of the intervention, the resistance the intervention might meet, and the integrity of the intervention.

Potential for effectiveness: The first question to be asked is whether the intervention fits you, your family, and the child. Are you comfortable with the selected plan, and does it address your understanding of the function of the child's target behavior? Next, does the intervention take into consideration the complexities of the home environment? Obviously, every family has its own limitations and expectations, as well as structure. For your planned intervention to be effective, you need to be able to implement it within the constraints of your home. And finally, have you adequately followed the steps in the systematic problem-solving approach provided here, so that you know the baseline of the target behavior, the context in which it occurs and the function it serves? If you can answer, "Yes," to these questions, your chosen intervention is much more likely to work. In addition, to be effective, the chosen intervention should be:

- developed specifically for the behaviors in question.
- appropriate for the situation.
- composed of the proper components.
- administered properly.
- given sufficient time to work (including time for any necessary modifications).
- powerful enough to initiate and maintain change over time.

Acceptability of an intervention: There needs to be a consensus among all the players (both parents, all children, and any other members of the family that interact on a regular basis with the child) that the planned intervention is acceptable. The parents need to be sure the intervention is compatible with their style, the child needs to "buy into" the plan, and both parents need to agree that a problem exists and that their child might benefit from this effort. When trying something new, you may find it helpful to ask others, especially other foster and adoptive parents and behavioral specialists, to think through your ideas and design with you. This is likely to increase your own sense that the planned intervention is a good idea that is acceptable to many.

Resistance and encouragement: The first step toward effective problem solving is the commitment to making changes in yourself and your home. The easiest way to do this is to work with your spouse and other children to improve the home climate. Sometimes you will meet with resistance as you find other foster or adoptive parents who have been beaten down by defeatist attitudes. You may find your spouse is resistant to change and feel frustrated that your efforts are futile. You may even have to overcome significant obstacles in yourself if you have an authoritarian approach to child rearing. You may have to battle your own tendencies for survival, your self-interest, and your anger and frustration as your child tests you on a daily basis.

As a foster or adoptive parent you face enormous pressures, and you often find yourself in a struggle to survive caring for a behaviorally disorganized child, often without even basic support. We realize how difficult it often is to retain your faith in yourself and your children. However, when you believe in yourself and your role as a parent, you will find the rewards—not only enhancing your own self-respect but earning the love and respect of your child—are enormous.

Integrity of the intervention: The intervention selected must be fully conceived, executable, and consistently implemented as planned. If you cannot follow through on the plan, then the integrity of the intervention will be significantly compromised, and it will be almost guaranteed to fail.

CASE STUDY: Tawanda

■ You want Tawanda to wait her turn to talk at home and to ask for help appropriately when she needs it while doing her homework, especially math. If she were able to do these things, Tawanda would be exhibiting much better impulse control. What interventions would be appropriate to help Tawanda with her impulsive talking and interrupting?

Case discussion

After explaining to Tawanda when it is appropriate to talk and when it isn't, you can tell her that each time she waits instead of interrupting, she will be given tokens she can collect to cash in for a treat or toy. You will remind her of this goal several times each day and acknowledge her when she waits to talk with you. You should be sure to help her know that attention will soon be directed her way if she can wait. Since math homework creates many of the behavioral difficulties for Tawanda, you will check with her frequently to make sure she understands the work and is able to complete it independently. You will encourage her to ask for help when she needs it. Additionally, you will obtain tutoring in math for Tawanda.

CASE STUDY: Chris

■ You now have a model for thinking about Chris' behavior and have some goals to help him learn new ways of self-regulation that will be more adaptive for him. What interventions would be most effective in helping Chris navigate transitions?

Case discussion

Chris appears to be typical of many drug-exposed children who have difficulty transitioning from one situation to another. After reading the information on transitions in a previous section, you realize that you have not been properly preparing Chris for transitions, and while most children adjust to them smoothly, Chris cannot. You develop a routine at home to warn Chris about a transition ten minutes ahead of time. At five minutes you provide a reminder. During transitions, such as preparing for dinner or going out in the car, you keep Chris close to you, putting a hand on his shoulder when you see him begin to lose control. When Chris is to have unstructured time at home, you will spend a few minutes with Chris, planning what he would like to do with his time. You also want to implement strategies that will teach Chris how to manage himself internally with calming strategies including deep breathing, putting his head down or leaving an over-stimulating situation instead of relying on others to control him.

▌▐

Step 6 : Communicate interventions to the child

This aspect of an intervention is easy to overlook but is an important ingredient for a successful intervention. All interested parties ("stakeholders") need to be fully informed about the plan and given opportunities to contribute and ask questions. To be successful, the intervention must be acceptable to the child, thereby increasing the probability that the appropriate behavior will occur. The need for acceptability applies at a broader level as well: Is it acceptable to the rest of the family? If an intervention is acceptable to all involved parties, then its chances of being supported and successful increase greatly.

Interventions should be thought of as positive both in intent and effect. It is important that the child be included in the process of defining an intervention, since he will be responsible for executing it. In talking with the child you must be nonjudgmental and begin the conversation by asking questions to understand his feelings and to clarify your perceptions of the problem and its meaning/function. You must then lead the child to understand his role in creating the problem and give him opportunities to identify ideas and/or respond to a proposed solution. At this point both the parent and the child will work together to set realistic goals and establish ways to evaluate progress.

The child's teacher is an integral part of any intervention effort. It is important to develop collaborative relationships with her early in the process. If you want the teacher to play a constructive role in the process, you need to remember that the goal is to find solutions to the problem, not someone to blame for it. Once you have developed a plan, ask the teacher to meet with you so you can share your ideas and beliefs. Allow her opportunities to question your plan and add any ideas she may have. Create the final plan together, so all the stakeholders can participate and feel ownership in the efforts. The child should be included in at least part of the meeting with the teacher, so he can see the mutual efforts and collaboration between home and school.

As you conclude the meeting, arrange to have the teacher send you a note each week to let you know how the intervention is going at school. Establishing this expectation will confirm a partnership between home and school.

CASE STUDY: Tawanda

▮ Now that you've decided on an intervention for the target behaviors, you need to communicate your ideas and strategies to Tawanda and her teacher. What would be important to point out in explaining the interventions to them?

Case discussion

It is important that you communicate your concerns and intervention strategies to Tawanda and her teacher in an objective and nonjudgmental manner, especially in light of the fact that Tawanda's behavior is irritating you. Tawanda should be told that, while you understand she is excited and wants to share her thoughts, her interruptions disturb both you and her siblings. You must allow Tawanda to help identify a meaningful reward. Tawanda's teacher agrees to support the reward system at school. You agree to communicate on a weekly basis with Tawanda's teacher in regard to her progress.

CASE STUDY: Chris

▮ You are now ready to communicate your ideas to Chris and his teacher to allow them opportunities to respond to your ideas and "buy into" these new interventions. What would be important in your communication to Chris and his teacher?

Case discussion

Chris must realize that you believe his behavior is not willful. Chris should be led to understand that sometimes he loses control but that there are ways he can learn to get himself under control. His teacher must be brought into the process of teaching Chris to manage his own behavior more effectively. The teacher and other school staff should be educated as to what regulatory problems are and how they should deal with them.

■ ■

Step 7: Implement selected interventions

The key to implementing your selected interventions is to continuously seek and take advantage of the teachable moments within the routine of the day. Usually, these teachable moments are most available after the child has had a positive experience: "Didn't homework go better tonight?"

Implementing the more formal aspects of the intervention requires planning. By this point you have identified the specific approach you will use, established the logical consequences or reinforcement to be used, and decided how and when to deliver them. Before you begin implementing the intervention you may want to think about the following:

- Do you have all the supplies (stickers, prizes, etc.) you will need?
- When will you start?
- How will you evaluate your progress?
- Reiterate your plan to the child in simple, positive terms.
- Point out that you believe the child can be successful and that this plan will help things go better at home and in school.
- Be sure to remind the child of what you expect of her.
- Be sure to remind the child of the reinforcement/consequence of her behavior.

- Provide an opportunity for questions. The child needs to feel like a partner in the process and understand how the two of you will work together.

After these preliminary steps, carry on the intervention as planned. As you implement your intervention there are some critical things you must remember:

1. *Don't deviate from your goals.* You have constructed a plan to address the most problematic behaviors. If there are some minor costs to developing the self-management capacity you are seeking, that may be all right for the short run because the real priority you've set will allow the child to succeed in the long run.

2. *Keep your eye on the prize for this child.* This may mean the child completes only half the math problems on his homework, but he does them carefully and accurately.

3. *Do not confuse consistency with rigidity.* You want the child to be successful because success breeds success, and chronic failure will ensure that your intervention also will fail. The child may need an extra reminder or chance to behave as desired. You may find that your initial plan is too difficult for the child, and you need to quickly lower your expectations so the child is successful. You can build back up to your original goals over time. Don't back yourself into a corner by declaring your plan as carved in stone. Give yourself some flexibility while remaining consistent in the execution of your stated plan.

4. *Use rewards as incentives.* Rewards serve as incentives for all of us to exert the extra effort to do something that is genuinely difficult. They help build new capacities in children by having them exert this extra effort and discover they can manage themselves in ways they didn't know they could. However, for a reward (or punishment) to work, it has to be

meaningful to the child. Some children will respond to verbal praise, others to stickers, others to treats and others to extra choices. Offering stickers to a child who couldn't care less about them will not give you the "payoff" you seek. The reward is not the intervention; it is a way to mark success.

5. *The name of the game is control.* It never feels good to be out of control, and this is true for children as well as adults. Children are frightened by the loss of control but often do not know how to avoid these experiences or regain control after an incident. There is a big built-in payoff to staying in control; it makes the child feel good.

6. *Be empathic.* Even as you set limits and manage behavior, you can empathize with a child's experience and emotional state. Thus, the child who is frustrated or over-excited will respond to the feeling that you understand him, even as you let him know his behavior (i.e., hitting, throwing, running around) is unacceptable. We cannot change the child's feelings, only the way he responds to the feelings. Couch your limit-setting language with empathy, "I see that you are feeling angry, but you may not hit your sister. When you calm down, let's talk about what to do when you feel angry."

7. *Be empowering; make sure the child experiences her own success.* Reminding the child, "I want you to have a good day because it makes you feel good and makes you happy," is critical. Reflecting this experience can help the child focus on her own internal rewards (i.e., "You must feel great about how well you did that!"). The sequence of events becomes:

   a. The child does what you want her to do
   b. You provide a positive consequence.
   c. You enhance her feelings of success, competence, and self-esteem.
   d. This increases the likelihood of the child's maintaining the appropriate behavior.

∎   *CASE STUDY: Tawanda*

∎   You are now ready to start your new plan to reduce Tawanda's frequent talking and interruptions. What do you need to prepare for implementation?

Case discussion

There are no special supplies needed for Tawanda other than the tokens and rewards that you have selected for reinforcement. You are going to evaluate your progress through the same tools that you used in collecting baseline information. You will remind Tawanda each day of the plan, and talk with her toward the end of the day for a few minutes about her success or difficulty that day.

                                                       CASE STUDY: Chris

∎   Chris' teacher is very enthusiastic about your ideas and plans to adapt some of them to her own classroom situations. She agrees that incentives often work with Chris to help him manage himself better. You decide to incorporate this into your plan. Are you prepared to implement the selected interventions?

Case discussion

Helping a child like Chris learn to regulate his own behavior may require a change in the way you think about Chris and your parenting style. Rather than seeing him as disobedient and "naughty," you understand that his behavior may be just as distressing for him. Your parenting style will change from being controlling to teaching how to control. You have posted a set of rules and logical consequences that are positive. You go over the daily schedule each morning and preview tomorrow's schedule at the end of the day. You have agreed to verbal reminders for prompting him about impending transitions. You have had a conference with his teacher to make her aware of Chris's regulatory problems, and she has agreed to reinforce your interventions when Chris is in the classroom. You have set up a chart that allows you and Chris to monitor his success each day with special privileges being offered as an incentive.

∎ ∎

Step 8: Evaluate and revise interventions

Give any intervention sufficient time to work,
ally at least two weeks. Remember that the targe
havior may increase at first; the child is testing
see if you will be consistent and stick with the
plan. If the intervention continues without
change for two weeks or longer, the behavior
usually will subside to levels lower than it was
before the intervention started. It is a rare occurrence when an intervention provokes the target behavior, but if it does, you may want to make a
change before the two-week period is up. Don't forget to remind the
child of the plan each day or before each situation that is likely to
create a problem.

If the intervention appears successful, evaluating it will not be a
problem. Use the same technique you used to establish the baseline,
and then compare the results. This comparison can help you explain to the child how the intervention is progressing and can be a
source of positive feedback for the child. However, if comparing the
data does not indicate success, you probably want to make some
changes in the intervention. You cannot always predict how a child
will react to a new intervention, and you may think of ways to improve your plan:

1. Return to the first step in the problem-solving process,
   whether you intend to choose a new intervention or to modify
   the existing one. Usually, as you review the early steps, you
   will identify the issues that require modification, thus making it easier to make appropriate changes.

2. Walk through the whole problem-solving process as before;
   repeat the process as many times as needed until you achieve
   success.

3. If a variety of attempts do not result in success, then you
   should seek consultation with an experienced professional.

Consultation is also a good source of support to review interventions that are working effectively to decide when they need modification or to be phased out.

As you work to determine if your intervention has been successful, make sure you have kept your eyes on the goals you initially set. If you change your own goals in midstream it is very difficult to gauge success.

After you've established the amount of progress the child has made, make sure you share information with the teacher. The same things that frustrate you often frustrate teachers, and hearing about the child's success can empower them to try different tactics at school. If your efforts have not been successful, then the teachers are likely to feel less critical of their own teaching failures and may be interested in trying new things in collaboration with you.

Once the child has mastered the new behavior, you can begin to phase out the intervention, or replace the target behavior with another challenging behavior the child has not yet mastered. The intervention may be reduced so it is less intrusive, and rewards or incentives can be phased out. Children should first be encouraged to monitor themselves and determine if they are deserving of the reward. They should begin to give themselves the reward for a job well done, rather than having it continue to come from an external agent. Rewards also can be phased out by providing a surprise reward at some unexpected time if the child has done a good job continuing to manage himself. You can remind him that he needs to maintain the behavior to get a surprise, and then once every week or two, you can provide this kind of reinforcement. At this point the child has mastered the new skill and is probably experiencing self-reinforcing payoffs, such as competence, improved relationships, and feeling more in control.

CASE STUDY: Tawanda

■ You have been implementing the intervention for a two-week period. You then spend three days collecting data about the frequency of Tawanda's interruptions and the amount of time she spends talking and disturbing her siblings. After looking at your new data about Tawanda's progress, are there revisions you would make in the interventions?

Case discussion

In looking at the evaluation collected over the past few days you feel you have had mixed success. Tawanda's interrupting and parroting you has decreased slightly. At school, her talking also has decreased and her math grades have improved. During the first two weeks of intervention she has waited to talk 15 times and has collected enough tokens for two special treats. You are not sure how the interventions are going at school because the teacher has not returned your call. You decide that there is enough progress to keep the intervention going, but you think certain areas need modification. You assign an older sibling to be a "study buddy" who will sit next to her and help her during homework time.

CASE STUDY: Chris

■ You have been doing all the things set out in your plan, and you've been talking through calming strategies with Chris when he seems close to losing control. How much progress could you expect to see in Chris during a two-week period?

Case discussion

You are disappointed because there is little progress in Chris' ability to control the volume of his voice, and, while there is a slight improvement, he still does not transition from one activity to another very well. However, there is an immediate positive change in his behavior at the dinner table. Although you have done your best to prepare Chris for transitions, the effect of your hard work is not as great as you had hoped.

Teaching self-regulation and control is a long process. You should not expect to see any great changes in Chris' behavior in two weeks. The important thing is to be consistent and stick to the plan. The more times Chris is prompted and reminded of strategies that will help him stay under his threshold of stimulation, the more he will be able to use those strategies to regulate his behavior. Your success in managing Chris' problems at dinner time leads you to believe you are on the right track in thinking he may have difficulty managing space. You think this may be a positive intervention for all the children and resolve to take steps to make the dinner table less crowded.

A Final Word

Thek are exciting times. We are learning more and more about early brain development and the way children learn. We now know that brain cells begin learning during fetal development, and the connections between the brain cells, which allow them to communicate with one another, grow at an astounding rate through the baby's first year of life. During this time, the sounds, sights, touches, smells and feelings that parents communicate to the child promote the growth of the neural pathways for emotions, speech and intellect. Your child learns language, abstract thinking, and becomes a social being through your playing with him. And, contrary to popular thought, it is not as important to teach young children their ABC's, numbers and colors, as it is to give them the emotional groundwork they need for lifelong learning.

More than anything, it is important to respect the dignity of the child and to help him feel worthwhile. Teaching a child to manage his own behavior rather than relying on the parents' controlling the behavior becomes a mechanism for reinforcement. When we give credit to the child for managing his own behavior, we emphasize that his success depended on something he did. Thus the success is more reinforcing and becomes not only a response but also a consequence. Our ultimate goal is to transform consequences into life-enhancing values. From the perspective of the *SORC* model of behavior, stimuli and the characteristics of the organism shape behavior, consequences maintain, refine, and ultimately define behavior.

We clearly do not know everything a child needs for optimum brain development. We do know, though, that prenatal drug exposure, neglect, abuse, lack of stimulation, emotional deficits and traumatic experiences can disrupt the wiring, leading a child into negative behaviors and feelings that last a lifetime. This is where foster and adoptive parents step in. All children are born ready to grow, both intellectually and emotionally. But their interaction with the world around them determines how that growth will proceed. That is why we must take whatever circumstances we are presented with when we bring a new child into our homes and provide the child with the kind of experiences that are protective and will promote successful development.

Brain development is not a simple matter of nature or nurture; nor does nature stop when nurture begins. The challenge to foster and adoptive parents, teachers, physicians, and anyone else who has a child in their care, is to provide an opportunity for growth to all children. Through love and comfort, through teaching and guiding, through managing and supporting, we can all make a difference in the life of a child.

■　　■　　■

ACKNOWLEDGEMENTS

Children's Research Triangle (CRT) is a not-for-profit organization dedicated to the healthy development of children and their families. CRT transfers the knowledge gained from research and clinical care into practice, providing comprehensive services to children and families through our clinical partner, the Child Study Center. There is an incredible team at Children's Research Triangle, each member of that team contributing invaluable knowledge and expertise for this book.

Kai Iaukea brings her classroom experience and skills to the development of strategies for teaching young children at risk. Amy Anson, Linda Schwartz, Margot Mahan, Craig McCall, Mary Sue Rudisill, and Kim D. Coleman are members of our treatment team, past and present, who have taught me so much about children's emotional, social, and cognitive development. Connie Blade shares pediatric duties with me and keeps us up to date with all the newest developments in children's health care. Dorothy Frooman makes sure we have an organized office to work in. Jackie Madison and Eric McKenzie lead our community outreach efforts, and Kimberly Thompson and Mary Schwitters make sure all the children and families feel welcome as they come into the center. Wei Chen Hung takes my ideas and turns them into documents that teach. Dale Simons handles all the organizational details and keeps things moving when my mind is elsewhere. Arthur Wildbrew edits meticulously, disallowing overblown metaphors and irrelevant passages. Rich McGourty drops pearls of wisdom with little effort and provides incredible insight into understanding difficult issues. These are the members of Children's Research Triangle who devote their working lives to taking care of the children and families who often have nowhere else to turn. I admire them greatly.

Most especially, I am grateful to my wife Carol for her interminable support for the last 32 years and to my children, Joel, Dorit, Ariel, and Gabriel, who taught me – and continue to teach me – how to be a father. Finally, my particular thanks go to the many foster and adoptive parents and their children who have come my way. You are special people.

Index

glossary

A

Aggressive behavior

A physical or verbal confrontation or behavior that is inappropriate to the situation and tends to violate the rights of others.

At-risk children

Children who have a greater probability of academic, social, emotional, behavioral, or developmental problems than most children, due to personal, family, or other factors.

Attention Deficit Hyperactivity Disorder/Attention Deficit Disorder

A behavioral pattern characterized by developmentally inappropriate levels of inattention, impulsiveness, and hyperactivity. Not all children with this condition show hyperactivity, but attention deficits are always present to some degree. Attention Deficit Disorder may exist with other disorders and is often confused with other problems.

Aversive

The degree to which an intervention requires more complex and negative procedures to produce an effect.

B

Baseline

Initial levels of behavior before intervention, in terms of frequency, duration, and/or intensity.

Behavioral contract

A verbal or written agreement between a child and adult that states what behavior(s) the child must demonstrate, the conditions under which those behaviors are to occur, and what the consequences of those behaviors will be.

Behavior

Observable physical action or verbal statement.

C

Consequence

In the *SORC* model, any immediate or distant event that results from a behavior, whether the event is desired (reinforcement) or undesired (punishment).

Contingency

The relationship between a stimulus, such as a positive reinforcement, and the appropriate behavior. The positive reinforcement is contingent (dependent) upon the child's performance of the appropriate behavior.

Contributing factors

The child's circumstances, experiences, and characteristics, which may or may not be as significant in directing the child's behavior as the home environment.

Control

Containing or inhibiting behavior, in contrast to management of behavior.

D

Deficit

An inability or inadequacy compared to other children. This may be a skill deficit (child does not have the skill to perform a behavior) or a performance deficit (child has the skill to perform a behavior, but does not do so when required).

Delinquent

Acting-out, noncompliance, under-controlled behavior.

Disruptive behavior

Inappropriate behavior that inter-rupts the routine and continuity of the home or classroom.

Drug

A chemical substance, either illegal or legal (including prescription medicine and alcohol).

Duration

Length of time a specific behavior continues.

E

Environment

Surroundings, specifically at home or in the classroom.

Externalizing behavior

Acting-out, under-controlled behav-ior, often characterized by noncom-pliance, defiance, aggressiveness, or similar behavior.

F

Facilitate

To make a strategy, activity, or developmental experience easier and more efficient.

Fetal Alcohol Syndrome

A combination of cognitive and/or behavioral deficits, poor growth, and abnormal formation of the face, resulting from prenatal exposure to alcohol.

Focus

Clear, directed attention.

Frequency

How often a documented behavior occurs in a specified period.

H

Hyperactivity

Under-controlled behavior, charac-terized by high levels of movement and activity, demonstrated in the home or classroom as difficulty in remaining seated or running excessively.

I

Immediate factors

Those factors having a direct relationship to current problems.

Implement

To initiate a developed and tested intervention in response to an identified behavior.

Impulsive behavior

Under-controlled behavior related to a low threshold for over-stimulation and a low tolerance for frustration, characterized by sudden outbursts.

Intensity

The severity of a behavior in terms of excessive frequency or duration and its impact on the child or others.

Intervention

Practical, effective strategies to be used by parents in the home or teachers in the classroom to address behavioral problems.

L

Longitudinal

Research conducted over an extended period with the same subjects.

M

Management

Maintaining children's appropriate prosocial behavior by establishing clear expectations, using developmentally appropriate practices, and arranging the physical environment to optimize on-task learning.

Manipulate

Purposefully moving objects, tools, or abstract ideas.

N

Negative punishment

The parent's contingent response to a child's inappropriate behavior, to lessen the behavior by removing a desired object, activity or privilege from the child.

Negative reinforcement

The parent's contingent response to a child's appropriate behavior, to increase the behavior by removing an undesired object, activity, or responsibility from the child.

Non-immediate factors

Factors having only an indirect relationship to current problems.

O

Off-task

Not focused on the appropriate learning activity.

On-task

Focused on the appropriate learning activity for prolonged periods of time without becoming easily distracted.

Organism

In the *SORC* model, the child's cognitive process that acknowledges, recognizes, and interprets the stimulus.

Over-controlled

Withdrawn, shy, and less assertive than the typical child; lacking personal energy for prosocial behavior to an extent that creates personal and social problems. Over-controlled behavior contrasts with under-controlled behavior.

Over-stimulation

Providing the child with more sensory input than he can "filter" or effectively manage.

P

Perinatal

Around the time of birth.

Positive punishment

The parent's contingent response to a child's inappropriate behavior, to lessen the behavior by placing an undesired object, activity or responsibility with the child.

Positive reinforcement

The parent's contingent response to a child's appropriate behavior, to increase the behavior by placing a desired object, activity or privilege with the child.

Prenatal

Pertaining to the gestation period; prior to birth.

Prenatally-exposed

Children whose mothers used cocaine, alcohol, or other drugs during pregnancy.

Prevention

Acting before an undesirable event to avoid the event's taking place.

Problem-solving

Attempting to understand the causes of problems, thinking about the factors involved, considering alternatives in an attempt to develop solutions, and being willing to try different approaches for long-term results.

Prompt

Physical or verbal action or comment used to assist a child in beginning an appropriate behavior or activity.

Prosocial

Behaviors effective in helping the child meet the demands of her setting, leading to more effective social and academic functioning.

Punishment

The parent's response to a child's inappropriate behavior in order to lessen the behavior.

R

Reinforce

To strengthen a behavior, i.e., to establish conditions in which a behavior is likely to increase in response to the child's receiving a desired event, object, or privilege.

Representational play

Play in which a child uses one object to represent another; e.g., a broom used as a toy horse.

Reprimand

A negative verbal statement directed at a child's misbehavior, designed to reduce or eliminate the behavior.

Response

In the *SORC* model, the child's behavior in relation to stimulus and interpretation of the stimulus. consideration and interpretation of the stimulus selects the individual's response from his repertoire of behaviors.

Ritalin

A prescribed form of amphetamines often used to treat children with Attention Deficit Hyperactivity Disorder.

S

Shutting-down

The way children respond to overload by shutting themselves off and attempting to block out any further environmental stimulation.

Solitary play

Playing alone, uninvolved with other children.

State regulation

The ability of the child to regulate his behavior in response to various environmental stimuli.

Stimulus

In the *SORC* model, any of a number of biological drives (hunger, thirst) or environmental factors (smell, sight) that set off a chain of responses that result in manifest behavior.

Substance

Cocaine, alcohol, tobacco, or other drugs.

T

Target behavior

Inappropriate behavior that is the focus of change.

Time out

A period of time in which the parent removes or reduces the child's opportunity to earn reinforcements, in response to the child's inappropriate behavior.

Transition

A period of change in activities or locations, in which the child is expected to maintain appropriate behavior throughout the change.

Under-controlled

Aggressive, acting-out, inattentive, or similar behavior that is disruptive to the progress of a child.

V

Violent

Under-controlled behavior in which the child endangers another individual or himself.

references

American Academy of Pediatrics, Committee on Pediatric AIDS. (2000). Identification and care of HIV-exposed and HIV-infected infants, children, and adolescents in foster care. *Pediatrics*, July 106(1), 149-152

American Academy of Pediatrics, Committee on Substance Abuse and Committee on Children with Disabilities. (2000). Fetal alcohol syndrome and alcohol-related neurodevelopmental disorders. *Pediatrics*, August 106(2), 358-361

American Academy of Pediatrics, Committee on Quality Improvement, Subcommittee on Attention-Deficit/ Hyperactivity Disorder. (2000). Clinical practice guideline: diagnosis and evaluation of the child with attention deficit/hyperactivity disorder. *Pediatrics*, May 105(5), 1158-1170

Aronson, J.E. (1998). Hepatitis vaccination imperative for families adopting from abroad. *The Bulletin of the Joint Council on International Children's Services*, Summer 1998, 5

Azuma, S.D. & Chasnoff, I.J. (1993). Outcome of children prenatally exposed to cocaine and other drugs: A path analysis of three-year data. *Pediatrics*, 92, 396-402

Benoit, T. C., Jocelyn, L. J., Moddemann, D. M., & Embree, J. E. (1996). *Romanian adoption: The Manitoba experience.* Archives of Pediatric and Adolescent Medicine, *150, 1278-1282*

Berman, L.C. & Bufferd, R.K. (1986). Family treatment to address loss in adoptive families. *Social Casework*, January 1986: 67.3-11

Biederman, J., Faraone, V.S., Monuteaux, M.C., & Feighner, J.A. (2000). Patterns of alcohol and drug use in adolescents can be predicted by parental substance use disorders. *Pediatrics*, October 106(4) 792-797

Bowlby, J. (1969/1982). Attachment and loss: Vol. 1. Attachment. New York, NY; Basic Books

Bowlby, J. (1973). Attachment and loss: Vol. 2. Separation. New York, NY; Basic Books

Bowlby, J. (1980). Attachment and loss: Vol. 3. Loss. New York, NY; Basic Books

Brodzinsky, D., & Huffman, L. (1988). Transition to adoptive parenthood. *Marriage and Family Review*, 12, 267-286

Chasnoff, I.J., Callaghan, M.A., Zeisz, J., Randolph, L., Nanos, A.M., & Blade, C. (1998). *Systems Integration: The Child Study Center Behavioral Health Project.* Chicago, IL; NTI Publishing

Chasnoff, I.J. Prenatal exposure to cocaine and other drugs: is there a profile? In Accardo, P.J., Shapiro, B.K., and Capute, A.J., (eds.) *Behavior Belongs in the Brain.* Baltimore, MD; York Press, 1997:147-163

Chasnoff, I.J., Anson, A., Iaukea, K. (1998). *Understanding the Drug-Exposed Child: Approaches to Behavior and Learning.* Chicago, IL; Imprint Publications

Chasnoff, I.J., Anson, A.R., Hatcher, R., Stenson, H., Iaukea, K.A. & Randolf, L.A. (1998). Prenatal exposure to cocaine and other drugs: Outcome at four to six years. *Annals of the New York Academy of Sciences*, 314-328

Chasnoff, I.J., Burns, W.J., Schnoll, S.H., & Burns, K.A. (1983). Phencyclidine: Effects on the fetus and neonate. *Developmental Pharmacology and Therapeutics*, 6, 404-408

Chasnoff, I.J., Burns, W.J., Schnoll, S.H., & Burns, K.A. (1985) Cocaine use in pregnancy. *New England Journal of Medicine*, 313, 666-669

Chasnoff, I.J., Griffith, D.R., MacGregor, S., Dirkes, K., & Burns, K.A. (1989). Temporal patterns of cocaine use in pregnancy. *Journal of the American Medical Association*, 161, 1741-1744

Chisholm, K. (1998). *A Three year follow-up of attachment and indiscriminate friendliness in children adopted from Romanian orphanages.* Child Development, 69(4), 1092-1106

Chisholm, K., Carter, M., Ames, E. W., & Morrison, S. J. (1995). *Attachment security and indiscriminately friendly behavior in children adopted from Romanian orphanages.* Development and Psychopathology, 7, 283-294

Coles, C.D., Platzman, K.A., Rashkind-Hood, C.L., Brown, R.T., Falek, A., & Smith, I.E. (1997). *A comparison of children affected by prenatal alcohol exposure and attention deficit, hyperactivity disorder.* Alcohol Clinical Experimental Research, *February, 21(1), 150-61*

Coons, C.E., Gay, E.C., Fandal, A.W., Ker,C., & Frankenburg, W.K. (1981). *The Home Screening Questionnaire Reference Manual.* Denver, CO; University of Colorado

Delaney-Black, V., Covington, C., Templian, T., et al. (2000). Teacher-assessed behavior of children prenatally exposed to cocaine. *Pediatrics*, October 106(4), 782-791

Eisen, L.N., Field, T.M., Bandstra, E.S., Roberts, J.P., Morrow, C., Larson, S.K., & Steele, B.M. (1991). Perinatal cocaine effects on neonatal stress behavior and performance on the Brazelton Scale. *Pediatrics*, 88, 477-480

Erickson, E.H., (1963 Revised Ed.). *Childhood and Society,* New York; Norton

Fahlberg, V. (1979). *Attachment and Separation.* Lansing, MI; Michigan Dept. of Social Services

Finkelstein, N., Kennedy, C., Thomas, K., & Kearns, M. (1998). *Gender-specific Substance Abuse Treatment.* Chicago; NTI Publishing.

Finnegan, L.P., Connaughton, J.F., Kron, R.E., Samuels, S.J. & Batra, K.K. (1975). Neonatal abstinence syndrome: Assessment and management. In Harbison, R.D., ed. *Perinatal Addiction*, New York; Spectrum Publications, 141-158

Frank, D.A., Bauchner, H., Parker, S., Huber, A.M., Kyei-Aboagye, K., Cabral, H., & Zuckerman, B. (1960). Neonatal body proportionality and body composition after in-utero exposure to cocaine and marijuana. *Journal of Pediatrics*, 117, 622-626

Fried, P.A., & Watkinson, B. (1990). 36-and 48-month neurobehavioral follow-up of children prenatally exposed to marijuana, cigarettes, and alcohol. *Developmental and Behavioral Pediatrics*, 11(2), 49-58

Goldstein, J., Freud, A., & Solnit, A.J. (1973) *Beyond the Best Interests of the Child*, New York, N.Y.; The Free Press

Green, Morris, ed. *Bright Futures: Guidelines for Health Supervision of Infants, Children and Adolescents.* Washington DC; National Center for Education in Maternal and Child Health

Greenspan, S. (1981). Psychopathology and Adoption in Infancy and Early Childhood. New York; International Universities Press

Goldfarb, W. (1945). Psychological privation in infancy and subsequent adjustment. *American Journal of Orthopsychiatry,* 15, 247-255

Haggerty, R.J., Roghmann, K.J., & Pless, I.B. (1973). *Child Health and the Community.* New York; John Wiley & Sons

Hamill P.V.V., Drizd T.A., Johnson C.L., et al. (1979). Physical growth: National Center for Health Statistics percentiles. *American Journal of Clinical Nutrition,* 32, 609-610

Hoksbergenk, R. A. C. (1990). Intercountry adoption coming of age in The Netherlands: Basic issues, trends and developments. In H. Altstein & R. J. Simon (eds.) Intercountry Adoption: A Seven Country Perspective. *New York; Praeger*

Hostetter, M.K., Iverson, S., Thomas, W., et al. (1991). *Medical evaluation of internationally adopted children.* New England Journal of Medicine, 325, 479-485

Howe, D. (1997). Parent reported problems in 211 adopted children: Some risk and protective factors. *Journal of Child Psychology and Psychiatry and Allied Disciplines,* 38 (4), 401-411

Hurt, H., Brodsky, N.L., Betancourt, L., Braitman, L.E., Malmud, E., Giannetta, J. (1995). Cocaine-exposed children: follow-up through 30 months. *Journal of Substance Abuse,* 7(3), 267-80

Johnson, D.E., Miller, L.C., Iverson, S., et al. (1992). The health of children adopted from Romania. *Journal of the American Medical Association,* 268, 3446-3451

Jones, K.L., Smith, D.W., Ulleland, C.N., &Streissguth, A.P. (1973). Pattern of malformation in offspring of chronic alcoholic mothers. *Lancet,* 1, 1267-1271

Katz, L.L. (1987). An overview of current clinical issues in separation and placement. The foster care dilemma. In Lieberman, Kenemore and Yost (eds.) *Child and Adolescent Social Work Journal,* 4, fall/winter

Koren, G., Nulman, I., Rovet, J., Greenbaum, R., Loebstein, M., & Einarson, T. (1998). Long-term neurodevelopmental risks in children exposed in utero to cocaine. The Toronto Adoption Study. In Harvey, J.A., Kosofsky, B.E., et-al (eds.) *Cocaine: Effects on the Developing Brain*, New York, NY; New York Academy of Sciences , Vol. 846, 306-313

Kuhl, W. (1985). *When adopted children of foreign origin grow up.* Osnabruck; Terre des Hommes

Kumpfer, K.L. (1996). Factors and processes contributing to resilience: The resiliency framework. In M. Glantz, J. Johnson, & L. Huffman (eds.) *Resiliency and Development: Positive Life Adaptations.* New York; Plenum

Lester, B.M., Corwin, M.J., Sepkoski, C., Seifer, R., Peucher, M., McLaughlin, S. & Golum, H.L. (1991). Neurobehavioral syndromes in cocaine-exposed newborn infants. *Child Development*, 62, 694-705

Levy-Shiff, R., Goldschmidt, I., & Har-Even. (1991). Transition to parenthood in adoptive families. *Developmental Psychology*, 27, 131-140

Littner, N. (1974). The challenge to make fuller use of our knowledge about children. *Child Welfare,* 1(53), 288-289

Littner, N. (1972) *Some Traumatic Effects of Separation and Placement,* New York; Child Welfare League of America

Mainemer, H., Gilman, L. C., & Ames, E. W. (1998). Parenting stress in families adopting children from Romanian orphanages. *Journal of Family Issues, 19(2),*164-180

Marcovitch, S., Goldberg, S., Gold, A., Washington, J., et al. (1997). Determinants of behavioral problems in Romanian children adopted in Ontario. *International Journal of Behavioral Development, 20(1), 17-31*

Masten, A.S, Best, K.M., & Garmazy, N., (1990). Resilience and Development: Contributions from the study of children who overcome adversity. *Development and Psychopathology,* (2), 435-444

Mattson, S.N., Goodman, A.M., Caine, C., Delis, D.C., & Riley E.P. (1999). Executive functioning in children with heavy prenatal alcohol exposure. *Alcohol Clinical Experimental Research*, 23(11), 1808-15

Mayes, L.C., Bornstein, M.H., Chawarska, K., & Granger, R.H. (1995). Information processing and developmental assessments in 3-month-old infants exposed prenatally to cocaine. *Pediatrics*, 95, 539-545

Miller, L.C., Kiernan, M.T., Mathers, M.I. & Klein-Gitelman, M. (1995). Developmental and nutritional status of internationally adopted children. *Archives of Pediatric and Adolescent Medicine*, 149, 40-44

Morrison, D.C., Cerles, L., Montaini-Klovdahl, L., & Skowron, E. (2000). Prenatally drug-exposed toddlers: cognitive and social development. *American Journal of Orthopsychiatry*, April, 70(2), 278-83

Morse, B., Idelson, R.K., Jacho, W.H., Weiner, L., & Kaplan, L. (1992). Pediatricians' perspectives on FAS. *Journal of Substance Abuse*, 187-195

Nulman, I., Rovet, J., Altmann, D., Bradley, C., Einarson, T., Koren, G. (1995). Neurodevelopment of adopted children exposed in utero to cocaine. *Journal of Development and Behavioral Pediatrics*, 16(6), 418-24; discussion 425-30

Oulellette, E.M., Rosett, H.L., Rosman, N.P., et al. (1977). Adverse effects on offspring of maternal alcohol abuse during pregnancy. *New England Journal of Medicine*, 297, 528-531

Ornoy, A., Michailevskaya, V., Lukashov, I., Bar-Hamburger, R., Harel, S. (1994). The developmental outcome of children born to heroin-dependent mothers, raised at home or adopted. *Canadian Medical Association Journal of Medicine*, (11), 1591-7

Provence, S. & Lipton, R. (1962). *Infants in Institutions: a Comparison of Their Development with Family-Reared Infants During the First Year of Life*. New York, NY; International Universities Press

The Report of the Carnegie Task Force on Learning in the Primary Grades. (1996) Carnegie Corporation of New York

Rutter, M. (1985). Resilience in the face of adversity: protective factors and resistance to psychiatric disorder. *British Journal of Psychiatry*, 147, 598-611

Sameroff, A.J., Barocas, R., Seifer, R. (1984). The early development of children born to mentally ill women. In Watt, N.F., Antony, E.J., Wynne, L.C., Rolf, J. (eds.) *Children at Risk for Schizophrenia: A Longitudinal Perspective.* Cambridge, England; Cambridge University Press

The Science of Early Childhood Development. (2000) Washington, DC; National Academy of Sciences

Seifer, R. & Sameroff, A.J. (1987). Multiple determinants of risk and invulnerability. In: Antony, E.J., Cohler, B.J., (eds.) *The Invulnerable Child.* New York; The Guilford Press, 51-69

Shedler, J., & Block, J. (1990). Adolescent drug use and psychological health: A longitudial inquiry. *American Psychologist,* 45, 612-630

Shonkoff, J.P. (1985). Social support and vulnerability to stress: a pediatric perspective. *Pediatric Annals,* 14, 550-554

Simms, M.D., Dubowitz, H., & Szilagyi, M.A., (2000). Health care needs of children in the foster care system. *Pediatrics,* October 106(4) 909-918

Singer, L.T., Garber, R., & Kliegman, R. (1991). Neurobehavioral sequelae of fetal cocaine exposure. *Journal of Pediatrics,* 119, 667-672

Skinner, B.F. (1971). *Beyond Freedom and Dignity.* New York, NY; Bantam Publishing

Sorenson, R.U., Leiva, L.E., & Kuvibidila, S. (1993). Malnutrition and the immune response. In Suskind, R.M. & Suskind L.S. (eds.) *Textbook of Pediatric Nutrition.* New York, NY; Raven Press, Ltd.

Spear, L.P., Kirstein, C.L., & Frambes, N.A. (1989). Cocaine effects on the developing central nervous system: behavioral psychopharmacological and neurochemical studies. In Hutchings, D.E., (ed.) *Prenatal Abuse of Licit and Illicit Drugs.* New York; *Annals of the New York Academy of Sciences,* 562, 290-307

Specter, M. (1997). AID's onrush sends Russia to the edge of an epidemic. *The New York Times, May 17*

Spitz, R. (1965) *The First Year of Life: A Psychoanalytic Study of Normal and Deviant Development of Object Relations.* New York; International Universities Press

Stanger C., McConaughym, S., & Achenbach, T. (1992). Three year course of behavioral/emotional problems in a national sample of 4- to 16-year olds: II. Predictors of syndromes. *Journal of the American Academy of Child and Adolescent Psychiatry*, 31, 941-950

Streissguth, A., Sampson, P., & Barr, H. (1989). Neurobehavioral dose-response effects of prenatal alcohol exposure in humans from infancy to adulthood. *Annals of the New York Academy of Sciences*, 562, 145-158

Takayama, J.T, Wolfe, E., & Couleter, K.P., (1998). Relationship between reason for placement and medical findings among children in foster care. *Pediatrics*, 101(2), 201-206

Tizard, B. (1991). Intercountry adoption: A review of the evidence. *Journal of Child Psychology and Psychiatry and Allied Disciplines*, 32 (5), 743-756

Van Horn, P. (1999). Understanding attachment disorders in infants and young children. *The Source*, 9 (3), 1-3, 16-17

Verhulst, F. C., Althaus, M. & Versluis-den Bieman, M.S . (1990). Problem behavior in international adoptees- I and II. *Journal of American Academy of Child and Adolescent Psychiatry*, 29, 94-103, 104-111

Wasserman, D.R. & Leventhal, J.M. (1993). Maltreatment of children born to cocaine-dependent mothers. *American Journal of Diseases of Children*, December, 147(12), 1324-8

Waters, E. & Deane, K.E. (1985). Defining and assessing individual differences in attachment relationships: Q-methodology and the organization of behavior in infancy and early childhood. In Bretherton & Waters (eds.) Growing points of attachment theory and research. *Monographs of the Society for Research in Child Development*, 50, (1-2, Serial No. 209)

Waters, E., Posada, G., Crowell, J., & Lay, K.L. (1993). *Is Attachment Theory Ready to Contribute to Our Understanding of Disruptive Behavior Problems: Development and Psychopathology*. Boston, MA; Cambridge University Press, 215-224

West, M. & Prinz, R.J. (1988). Parental alcoholism and childhood psychotherapy. *Psychological Bulletin*, 102, 204-218